A Stroll on the Moors

A Stroll on the Moors

Two Wild Weeks on Dartmoor

Second Edition

Mark Newman

A Stroll on the Moors – Two Wild Weeks on Dartmoor
Copyright © 2019 Mark Newman
All rights reserved

First published 2019
This second edition published 2020

Independently published via Kindle Direct Publishing

Cover photography/design and interior artwork by Mark Newman

ISBN 9798699506170

Mark Newman asserts his moral right to be identified
as the author of this work

Except by those means expressly permitted by Kindle Direct Publishing under license of
the copyright owner, no part of this publication may be reproduced, stored
in a retrieval system, or transmitted in any form or by any means, electronic,
mechanical, photocopying, recording, or otherwise, without prior
written permission of the copyright owner.

This book is sold subject to the condition that it shall not, by way of trade
or otherwise, be lent, re-sold, hired out or otherwise circulated in any form
of binding or cover other than that in which it is published and
without a similar condition including this condition being imposed
on the subsequent purchaser.

Contents

Prologue: The Traits-Triangle and the Thieving Squirrels 7

Chapter One: King of my Castle 12
Chapter Two: Paths 36
Chapter Three: Parasites 62
Chapter Four: Sustenance 79
Chapter Five: Relative Luxury & Momentous Moments 102
Chapter Six: Close Encounters 124
Chapter Seven: Isolation 144
Chapter Eight: Water and Technology 162
Chapter Nine: The Housing Inspector 177
Chapter Ten: Best Laid Plans 191

Epilogue: A Question Answered 211

About the Author 218

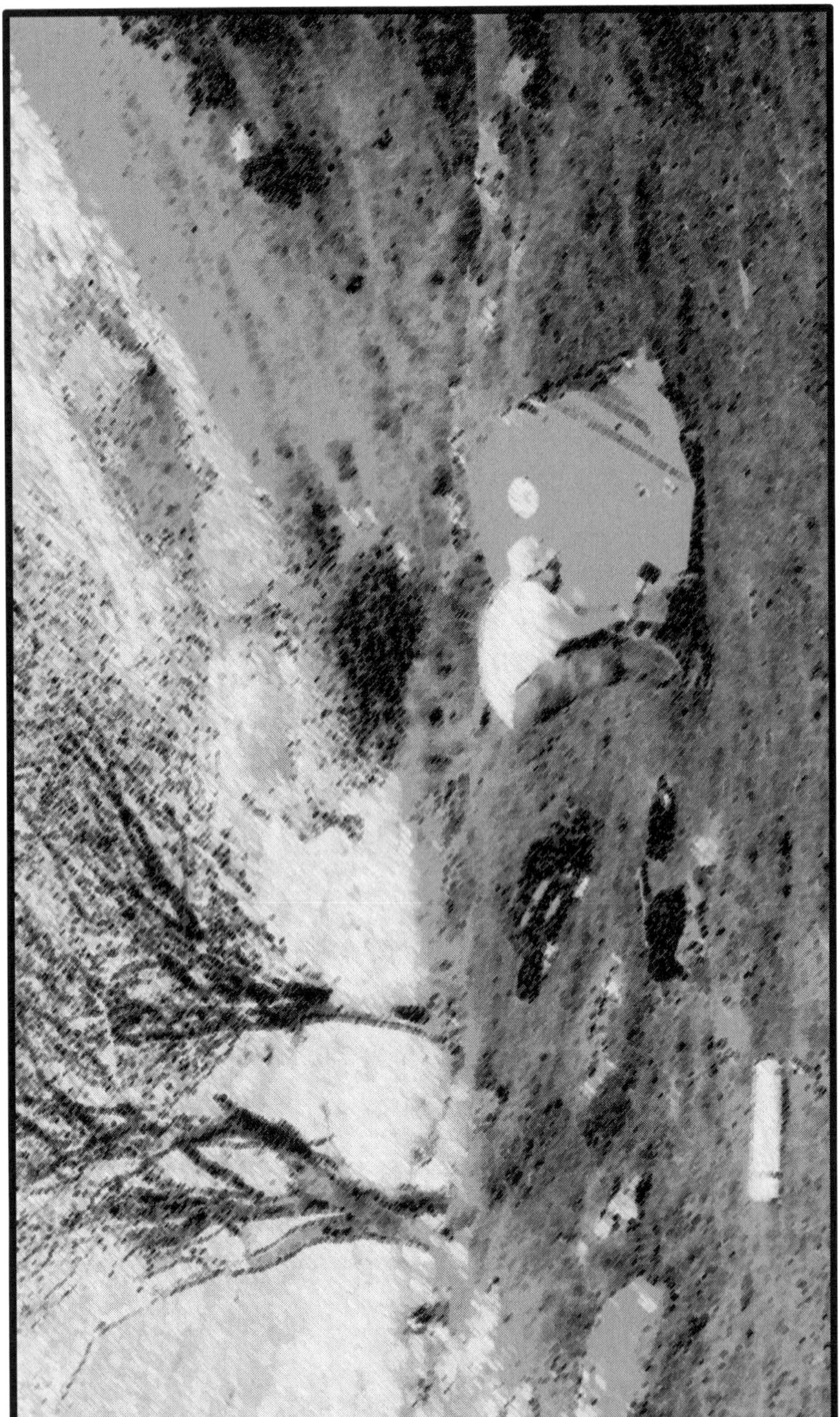

Prologue: The Traits-Triangle and the Thieving Squirrels

Gazing around this tiny, cluttered tent, where barely a square inch of the groundsheet is visible, I wonder how on earth I managed to cook inside the thing during its last use. I guess Dartmoor forced me to exercise a little more self-discipline and organisation than usual. Not much more, but a little.

Self-discipline. Organisation. Those are two personality traits I've always struggled to balance. I would, though, call myself a decent *planner* (or do I really mean 'dreamer'...?). Whilst there may be a fine line between these attributes, in my book they don't always sit well together. Regarding the latter two, planning is quite a broad term, isn't it? It's the successful execution of the plans that demands organisation. But when these three skills do come together in harmony, they form what I like to call the 'Traits-Triangle' (I can just hear the psychology academics calling to me now). I'm a man with many aspirations – but if I'm to succeed at more of them I probably need to work on my own Traits-Triangle.

I write this on a blustery autumnal afternoon, using the pen that slides out of my Swiss Army Knife. Most of the stuff scattered around me I also heaved across Dartmoor, crammed into my bulging 85-litre backpack (although, a little fraying of the straps aside, that backpack is still going strong, and right now is performing additional duties as a writing table. Not a great one, I'll admit, but it's doing the job).

Thanks to the constant roar of wind through the nearby oak trees, providing a generous smattering of acorns over the roof of my tent,

I barely slept last night. As a result, these words are coming to me a little laboriously.

I'm spending eight days and nine nights camping a mile or so from the village of Hathersage, in the heart of the Peak District National Park. I wouldn't ordinarily be using my tiny backpacker tent for a regular camping trip. However, my preferred accommodation – my far more spacious three-berth tent – was ruined by marauding squirrels last year. On more than one occasion I returned from my daily hikes to discover the little buggers had audaciously gnawed through the roof netting to nibble at my supply of chocolate bars. Though perhaps I had only myself to blame for choosing quite a nutty variety?

In any case, their wanton vandalism, along with the fact that I'd ripped the tent bag not long after arriving at the campsite, rendering the thing rather challenging to pack away and carry home, was enough to persuade me to stuff it into a bin as I exited the place.

That was something of a heart-breaking experience; of all the tents that had come and gone over the years, that one had served me the most faithfully. Such an ending for it seemed undignified. To compound this tragedy I also forgot to retrieve my tough-as-nails rock pegs from the thing before disposing of it.

That little incident had also occurred in the Peak District, a little over 12 months ago. I've therefore kept a beady eye on the squirrels I've observed scampering along the drystone walls of *this* site since my arrival. I've also deprived myself of chocolate bars. Hopefully the deluge of acorns will keep any would-be-thieves busy.

You may be curious as to why I've confined myself to my tent as opposed to getting out there into the great outdoors. Well, quite simply, I'm knackered. And not just through lack of sleep. I'm halfway through my stay, and three consecutive days of hillwalking, along with the preceding one spent hulking all my gear over a mile from the train station, have taken their toll on my feet.

Or perhaps that makes a handy excuse. Perhaps I'm illustrating, again, the absence of one of those vital skills required to keep my

Traits-Triangle from collapsing. After all, during my Dartmoor hike I couldn't simply take a day off. I had a schedule to keep. Quite a slack schedule, admittedly, but a schedule nonetheless, and back then I was carrying a ridiculously heavy load *every day*. But whilst I was in far from what you might call a peak state of fitness for that undertaking, I still weighed over a stone less than I do now, two-and-a-bit years on.

Anyway, that's enough rambling from me. It's time to nip outside for another squirrel patrol.

Just one more thing. If you're reading this whilst planning your own hike across those moors, then I feel duty-bound to point out that this is no guidebook. Not in a practical sense, anyway. Neither will you find any 'advice' as such on the subject of wild camping; my virgin attempt was not one to be emulated.

Crucially, what I hope you will discover, woven through my account of the landscapes I traversed and the challenges I faced, is some idea of how you might feel as you create your own memories of Dartmoor.

So, grab your walking boots and poles (the latter is another item I should've packed) and let's go.

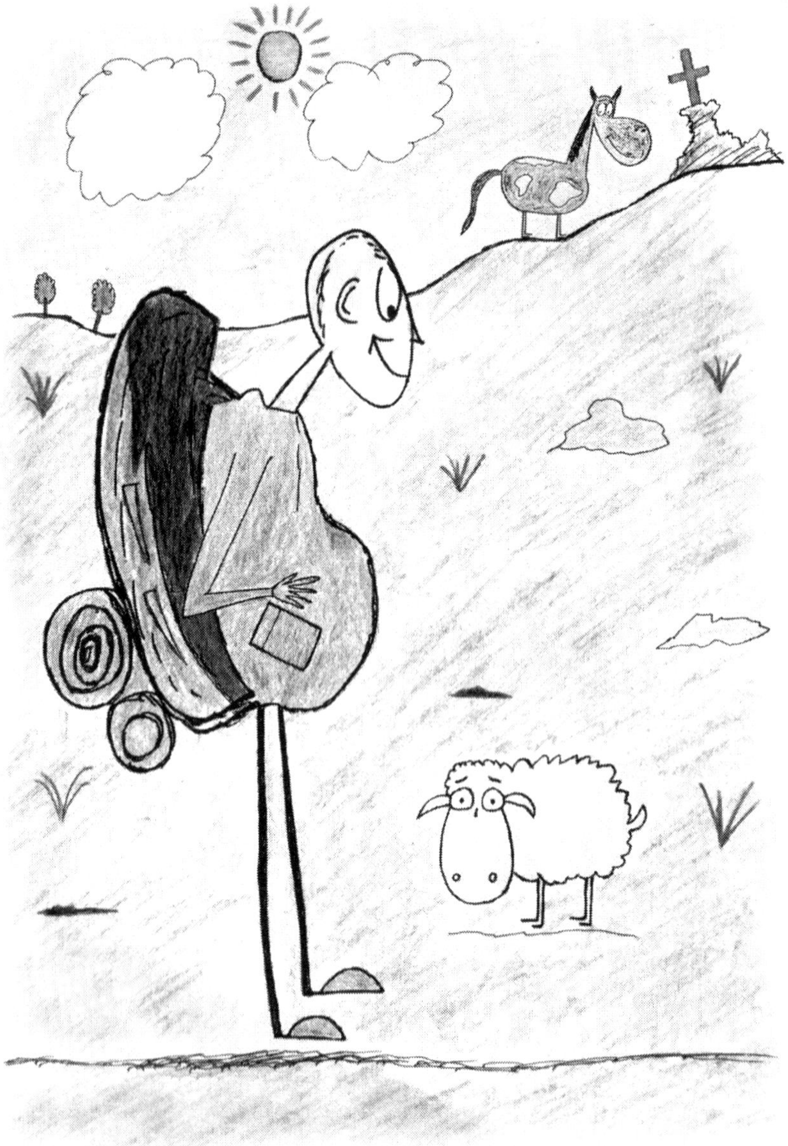

THE DRY WEEK

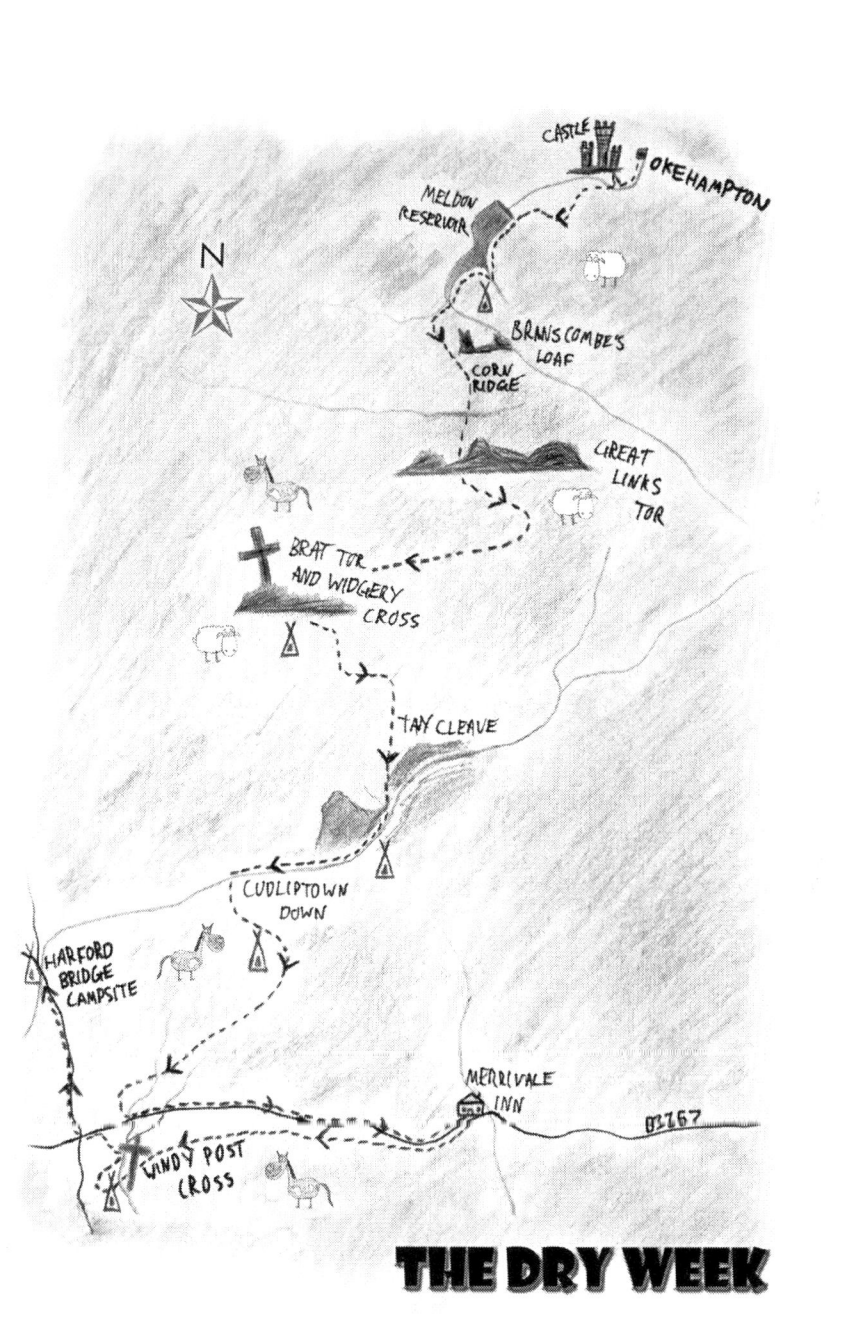

Chapter One: King of my Castle

Okehampton to Meldon Reservoir

Wiry branches clawed at the roof of the bus as it rattled through the Devonshire countryside; this road had clearly been built with smaller vehicles in mind. A hazy veil, courtesy of a dusty film covering the windows, attempted to shield my view of the lush trees lining the roadside. Occasionally those trees parted, revealing a teasing flash of the landscape beyond – each view wilder than the last. The classic, picture-postcard images of rural England I'd observed after leaving Exeter were quickly morphing into rolling swathes of straw-coloured hills and pristine moorland, capped here and there by curious rock formations – the Dartmoor Tors.

The bus was taking me to the small town of Okehampton – the gateway to the northern edge of Dartmoor National Park. This destination would be like nowhere I had visited before, and the realisation that I was almost at the start of my adventure sent a shiver of excitement cascading down my spine.

From Okehampton I would hike down the western side of the moor, reaching my mid-way point after six days: a campsite near the village of Peter Tavy. There I would bask in two days of relative luxury before returning to the moorland for another week. My arrival at Ivybridge – the southern counterpart of Okehampton – would conclude my hike, where a cosy room in a B&B awaited me.

Though by no means an expert, I regarded myself as someone who was competent in the outdoors, and a confident camper. I'd done quite a bit of it, after all – pitching up in Scotland, the Lake District, Northumberland, Snowdonia, and the Brecon Beacons over the years. But I had never camped *wild*. Surely then, with the inclusion of that extra element, this trip would trump all of my previous tenting adventures. Not that I was denigrating any of those experiences; attached to all of them, even those in which my plans had gone awry or the weather had been unforgiving, were fond memories.

Near Beddgelert, in Snowdonia, a few years back, I'd endured torrential rain, day and night, for nearly a week. My pitch ended up so swamped that at one point my groundsheet resembled a waterbed, rippling at my slightest motion, to the point where I half-expected to be swept away in the middle of the night. Amazingly my mud-clogged tent held up for the whole week, but when the time came to leave I couldn't bring myself to attempt packing it away. So I chucked it into a skip on my way out (that was the second of three occasions over the years in which I've ended up ditching my tent).

But I still went home with a smile on my face; camping isn't camping without the rain.

For this trip, though, I wanted to really test myself. I wanted to prove that travelling to faraway exotic lands to find a bit of adventure was unnecessary. I wanted to be somewhere totally alone and totally self-sufficient, in a landscape totally new to me. For those reasons I set my sights on one of England's numerous moorlands. Since camping wild was a key element of my trip, Dartmoor was the logical choice of destination – being the only part of England and Wales where wild camping is legally permitted (although the enforcement of and compliance with this law is a hot topic of debate amongst campers. We'll explore those legalities later). I also had all the time I needed to complete my adventure, having just given up my brain-numbing temping job in a call-centre.

But with my Traits-Triangle teetering precariously as usual, whilst planning my hike I hadn't fully considered the fact that this would be my first taste of *wild* camping. As well as all my usual gear, there would be extra equipment to consider taking along. Not exactly essential items, but certainly gadgets worth packing. However, most of the pack-space that should have been reserved for those extras had been hijacked by my camera gear. Then, of course, there were certain practical considerations to bear in mind. The kind of considerations that did not come to bare on any campsite...

But of far greater concern than those matters was the amount of weight I would be carrying; never before had I hiked anywhere carrying my entire camping gear, every day, for almost two weeks solid. On the other hand, whilst far from being the ultimate specimen of hulking masculinity, I was under no delusion that I was undertaking some great feat of human endurance. Whilst planning my route I reckoned my entire trek would cover no more than sixty miles – averaging a measly four per day. That's right: *four miles per day*. Nevertheless, factoring in the terrain and the weight I would be carrying, this hike would still be the most physically challenging venture I had ever committed to (and remains so to this day).

I know many people wouldn't rate a hike on Dartmoor as their ideal vacation – but we don't all look for the same thing in a holiday, do we? If all you desire is to sprawl out on a beach, getting frazzled by endless sunshine, then clearly Dartmoor isn't going to make an appearance in your top-ten of destinations. But when I go on holiday, the last thing I want to do is confine myself to a beach. And the fact that my skin only ever goes from alabaster white to lobster pink has nothing to do with it. I go on holiday to explore and to take photos. I'd become hooked on this hobby over the past couple of years, and after expanding my camera kit I was itching to find new locations in which to hone my skills. I was confident that Dartmoor would serve its purpose in that respect.

Dartmoor wasn't to be the be-all and end-all of this adventure, either. After a brief rest at Ivybridge I would be heading further south, for a ten-day trek along the South West Coastal Path. So altogether I would be spending the best part of a month exploring and photographing some of the wildest and most beautiful regions of Southwest England.

My family, particularly my mum and brother, hadn't exactly shared my enthusiasm on hearing my plans.

'Watch you don't get mugged!' That was my brother's only advice. Who did he think might be out there, waiting to mug unsuspecting hikers in the middle of some of the most remote moorland in the country?

As for my mum, she'd demanded I send her a text message once I'd arrived at the train station in Exeter. And another when I got off the bus in Okehampton. And another once I'd safely reached my first camping location. She only stopped issuing such demands after I pointed out that any phone signal would most likely desert me up on the moor. I would not be wasting precious battery power either, so would send her and my brother one message each when I was about to leave Okehampton.

Now, as the grey mosaic of an urban sprawl began to replace those intriguing views, that time appeared to be soon upon me. Some of my fellow passengers began to fiddle with their bags and walking sticks, which suggested an imminent arrival at a bus stop.

I took out my ordnance survey map and readied my backpack into its mounting position. My camera gear took up a sizable chunk of its capacity. This consisted of not just the camera, but three lenses, a camcorder, a tripod, and assorted accessories and spare batteries, all safely protected in a compartmentalised backpack – within my main pack. Crammed around this was two weeks' worth of food, clothing, my camping stove and gas, and a few other bits and pieces of gear. My sleeping bag had been afforded its own compartment at the bottom of the pack. Finally, strapped to the outside, were my sleeping mat and tent.

I had no idea how much this lot weighed – I only knew that bicep-power alone was insufficient to raise the ensemble more than six inches off the ground. Therefore, standing with my full kit hanging off my back for the first time, at six 'o' clock that morning, had involved getting onto all fours on the floor of my flat. Thankfully though, my transport hadn't been too crowded, so by keeping the pack perched next to me, sliding in and out of the straps before hauling myself to my feet, I'd so far managed to avoid any embarrassing incident.

Most of the passengers suddenly stood up and the bus pulled over. Once the others had alighted I followed them down the aisle, clutching my map as my pack bumped against the backs of seats.

Trying my best to avoid looking like a tourist – a rather pointless notion considering my baggage – I stepped out onto Okehampton's bustling High Street. I was dressed in a chequered black-and-white shirt over a white tee-shirt (beneath which a compass hung around my neck). Beige, ultra-lightweight trousers covered my chalk-white legs, accompanied by brown, nearly-new hiking boots. A matching canvas hat protected my bald bonce from the mid-day sun, which blazed fiercely with barely a cloud in the sky.

Eager to escape the jostling crowds, I buckled my waist-strap and set off, following the quickest route on the map that would lead me to a trail marked as the West Devon Way on the outskirts of town.

Halfway there I paused on a quiet side street, removing my shirt and tying it around my waist. I doubted that I'd need it for the remainder of the day, but there was no room for it in my stuffed pack. Taking a swig of water from my bottle, I remembered my mum's demand for a running commentary of messages. After considering my response, I sent her and my brother the following reassurance:

'About to head up onto the moors now. Might not have signal again for a couple of weeks so you'll just have to hope I can stay alive long enough to reach the next town.'

A minute later my brother replied with a four-word instruction to enjoy myself and be careful. My mum responded in a similar fashion, with the added caveat that I was to ring her if I got into trouble, and she and my step-dad would come and pick me up.

Clearly she'd glossed over the part about having no phone signal. I gave a wry smile at her glowing endorsement of my hiking skills – then headed south.

The West Devon Way is a 37-mile trail running from Okehampton to Plymouth. I would be following its first couple of miles to get up onto the moor. But as keen as I was to leave the town behind, I'd decided to take a slight detour to visit the remains of Okehampton Castle: a medieval ruin situated along the banks of the West Okemont River. So, shortly after joining the West Devon Way, I turned off where the path merged with a route marked as the Two Castles Trail.

About a mile from the bus stop I paused for another rest, taking a seat on a bench; prior to this day the furthest I'd ever walked bearing this kind of load was a few hundred metres between a bus stop and a campsite reception. After pushing on I crossed a footbridge over the river, then shortly after reached the castle entrance. I waited at a ticket kiosk behind an Australian-accented couple and their boisterous little boy, whilst the steward gave them travel directions.

My appearance seemed to have a somewhat calming influence on the child; almost immediately he paused his incessant jigging and tugging at his mother's hand, glaring up at me in a way that only a child would. My smile was sufficient to revert his attention back to his parents, though, who had remained oblivious to my presence. The couple eventually ran out of questions and departed with their offspring.

I paid the entry fee, which included the provision of an audio-descriptive track via a headset. Then the steward attempted to sell me a programme, followed by an annual membership of English Heritage, which offered 'unlimited entry to over 400 historic sites across the country'. I politely declined both offers.

'Would you like to leave your bag in here?' he then asked. 'You don't want to be humping it around up there, there's a fair few steps.'

I hesitated as my camera gear flashed through my brain. In monetary terms, the value of the lot was in the region of £1,200, and none of it was insured. Amongst my many jobs over the years I'd had a fair bit of experience in the insurance industry, and was well aware of the ream of small print insurers could rely on to get out of paying a claim. Out of principal, therefore, I never bothered to insure anything. As far as camera equipment goes, £1,200 certainly isn't expensive. But my gear represented much more to me than money. Over the past two years, photography had become my biggest and, frankly, my only passion in life. Without my camera, this hike would be virtually pointless. That was the reason for my hesitation; never letting my gear out of my sight had become second nature – I was casting no aspersions as to the steward's intentions. I also noted his point about humping my huge pack around the castle, especially as I observed the back-breaking climb to the castle's most prominent feature: the look-out tower.

Accepting the offer, I followed his gesture to a door at the side of the kiosk. Now I just had to get the thing off my back. Fortunately, the steward opened the door to reveal a hard chair. I slid the pack down the wall onto it, trying my best to disguise my struggle, then extracted my arms from the straps. The steward offered me a look of sympathy.

'Are you heading up to the moor?' he asked, adjusting the waist of his green jumper, which was decorated with the National Trust logo across the chest. He clearly wore this garment with pride, but on a day like this, sat in this cramped, wooden sweatbox all day, he must have been roasting in it.

'Yep, hopefully,' I replied, throwing in a chuckle.

'Well you've got the weather for it.' A grin stretched across his ruddy cheeks. 'I'm a bit jealous of you, to be honest. Are you going far?'

For some reason I was reluctant to divulge my plans, but somewhat distracted by the dull ache already nestling between my shoulder blades, I found myself confessing to him. 'I'm heading up to Meldon first, then working my way down to Ivybridge.' His grin faltered slightly.

'Oh, right,' he replied, bringing a sense of closure to our conversation as I extracted my camera and wide-angle lens from my pack. He then handed me a set of headphones, attached to which was a small MP3 player to provide the audio guide.

Leaving him as custodian of my belongings, I thanked the steward and donned the headset, then joined the dozen or so other tourists wandering amongst the ruins.

Okehampton Castle was once the largest such structure in Devon. Its earliest features date back to shortly after the Norman Conquest, and in the fourteenth century the finished castle became the official residence of the Earl of Devon: a man named Hugh Courtenay. Following the Wars of the Roses, and a controversial beheading of one of the Courtenay clan, the castle was abandoned and gradually fell into a state of ruin. In this dilapidated condition it remained until ownership transferred to the government in the 1960s. Major restorations and archaeological surveys followed, leading to the current management overseen by English Heritage.

That was the gist of the audio tour – and as much of it as my ears could take. I preferred to use my imagination rather than have all the castle's secrets blabbed out by the grandiose voice of an anonymous actor. But soon I began to wonder if I should have left the description running, for I couldn't help feeling slightly underwhelmed as I strolled amongst the grey walls of granite.

My indifference gave way to painful embarrassment when I failed to duck whilst passing through a low archway, bashing my scalp against the stone. Other than giving an immediate, involuntary grimace, I dismissed the incident as if nothing had happened – whilst inwardly cursing as my skull began to throb. Hopefully I wasn't about to require the use of my first aid kit already.

I spent a little over half an hour exploring both the ruins and the pretty little buttercup-filled meadow at the rear of the castle, concluding my visit with the steep climb up the huge mound of earth (or motte) to the remains of the tower. In contrast to the rest of the castle, this certainly was worth the visit – especially gazing up the teetering stack of crumbling stone at the top of the steps. This appeared to lack any substantial support from any of the surrounding walls, yet still stood tall and proud, keeping watch over the town.

After circling the tower I perched at the edge of the grassy bank to sample the views: to the north-east, Okehampton nestled before the green hills I'd passed through on the bus. To the south, the path of the river snaked up through the moorland hills, towards which I gazed curiously, pondering over where I might be spending the night. My only camping criteria was to be as close to Meldon Reservoir, located a few miles south-west of the town, as possible.

That whack on the head had been a hard one. The ache was slowly passing, but contrasted sharply with a teasing itch at the point of impact. I removed my hat and placed an index finger on the offending spot. I felt something sticky, then winced as a sting filtered through my skull. Expecting to see blood, an examination of my finger revealed a few blobs of a viscous, yellow goo. A scab was forming. That was fine with me; it was just a minor bump, evidenced also by the fact that none of my fellow tourists had stopped me in my tracks, urging me to seek medical attention as blood poured from my scalp. I flopped my hat back on loosely so as not to hinder the scab in its formation, then headed back down the steps.

It was time to get up onto Dartmoor.

I collected my pack and rejoined the West Devon Way, quickly leaving the town behind. Patches of woodland offered some precious shade as my elevation steadily increased. My route then crossed a golf course, where, keen to avoid sustaining a second head injury that afternoon, I kept my eyes peeled for any wayward balls.

Perhaps due to the absence of any crowd to blend into (although I recalled what little blending had taken place, despite the crowds, as I'd stepped off the bus), I felt more self-conscious here than I had in the town-centre. Or maybe the absence of any trees – for both shade and concealment purposes – had contributed more to my sense of apprehension as I cut across the fairway. I passed one or two golfers, who greeted me politely but seemed slightly baffled by my presence.

My route then led me across a stretch of farmland, where I paused at the earliest opportunity to take a break in the shade of a huge tree. Then I headed along a few country lanes and tracks.

Before reaching the reservoir I wanted to sample the views from Meldon Viaduct, which passed right over my route. But on arriving at the bottom of this massive web of steel an hour or so after leaving the castle, I discovered that getting to the top would demand a climb of a few hundred feet up a steep, winding path, skirting around one of the two concrete struts that supported the structure.

By this point, sweat patches decorated most of my tee-shirt and my bare forearms glistened. I rarely wear white tee-shirts in public. Not only because white clothing accentuates large waistlines, but also on account of how my nipples have always been almost permanently erect – thus appearing slightly indecent through white clothing (a 'friend' at high school had assigned me the rather unfortunate alias of 'Pop-Tits' in light of this slight peculiarity). Right there and then, though, as I willed my legs to carry me up the hill, I couldn't care less what anyone thought of my nipples.

By the time I reached the top, beads of sweat were rolling down my forehead, stinging my eyes. Offering a sliver of consolation, most of the zig-zagging climb had been completed in the shade.

As I emerged from the trees, legs wobbling, back into the blazing sunlight, I was greeted by a middle-aged woman, dressed in beige combat shorts and a white vest-top.

'Glad I'm not carrying that!' she boldly stated, nodding towards my pack, smiling politely but without stopping. I appreciated her sentiment, but all I could muster in response was a confused grimace of resignation, followed by a feeble smile. Her expression turned to one of sympathy, then she continued her walk along the track that crossed the viaduct, sparing me from using up my laboured breaths in conversation.

With the assistance of a low wall alongside the track, I detached the monster from my back, extracted my camera gear, and then shunted it behind a bin.

Feeling ever-so-slightly faint, I shuffled out onto the 165-metre span of the viaduct, lifting my arm to wipe another trickle of sweat from my temple. Halfway across I paused and turned – taking in my first majestic view of Dartmoor.

The most striking feature, just under a kilometre away, was Meldon Dam. Up until this point I'd been permitted only glimpses of it here and there, poking out from between the trees as I'd neared the viaduct. Its unnatural, concrete bulge, wedged into the valley, somehow blended into the scene perfectly. The West-Okemont River emerged from its base, though only a vague indication of its course was visible through the trees that smothered the valley floor.

The dam concealed the reservoir behind it, but the barren expanse of moorland beyond rolled on to the horizon like green and brown velvet. Bracken, gorse and hawthorn trees peppered the hills either side of the dam, with many of the latter sprayed with white blossom. Those hills climbed a little higher than where I now stood, and to the left of the dam, maybe a kilometre away, what I assumed was Meldon Quarry cut a huge, grey scar into the hillside.

A gently-sloping section of the valley, a few hundred metres in front of me, was designated a picnic area on the map. Sunbathers and picnickers lay sprawled out on the grass, making the most of the glorious weather.

I later learned that the feat of Victorian engineering upon which I stood had taken three years to build, serving the former London and South Western Railway until the late 1960s, when falling passenger numbers prompted the closure of the line. Material extracted from nearby Meldon Quarry continued to be transported across the viaduct until the 1990s, when it was deemed no longer strong enough to support rail traffic. The viaduct now forms part of the Granite Way; an 11-mile trail running from Okehampton to the village of Lydford, along the western edge of the national park.

A couple of cyclists approached, breaking the silence with snippets of chatter and the whirring of bicycle chains, before pausing to share my view. After a minute or two of camera-clicking they sped off, leaving me alone on the viaduct once more. Although my fatigue had left me as I'd surveyed the valley, I could have stayed there all afternoon to lap up this visual treat – and I hadn't even reached the moor yet. Already, a significant benchmark had been set for my expectations. But Meldon Reservoir was waiting. Torn between the views and my desire to dive head-first into that moorland, I forced myself to return to the West Devon Way, then pushed on.

Not long after, I arrived at the picnic area, passing alongside a few small, dilapidated buildings set in front of the quarry. Like the viaduct, this quarry had played a vital role to local infrastructure during the industrial revolution, producing hundreds of thousands of tonnes of ballast every year for the railways. But owing to financial pressures and the falling demand for its rock, Meldon Quarry closed operationally in 2011.

The cattle-grazed hills rose sharply on the other side of the river, slices of which now appeared through the scrub. Across this gentler side of the valley, sheep competed with humans for patches of shade amongst the gorse and hawthorn trees, and as I passed a car park, a flock of them darted away at the sound of my boots crunching on the gravelly path.

I wanted to take another break, especially after finding a charming little stream running down the hillside. But approaching its banks led to the discovery of more sunbathers who had already staked their claims on that spot. There was nowhere at all for me to rest, in fact – through either lack of space, or the absence of any rock or tree that would assist in getting my pack off and on again. So on I went, continuing along the hillside towards the dam, with the path gradually steepening. By this point I'd left the West Devon Way some time ago, though exactly where or when, I was unsure of.

Once the walkers, sunbathers and sheep were all behind me, I came across a shady spot under a tree, so I leaned back against the hillside and slid out of my pack.

Here I relaxed, perched on a little shelf of grass, for over an hour, watching wispy clouds drift slowly across the sky. Trickling water, the twitter of birds, and the occasional bleating of sheep underscored my rapture. The soft scent of hawthorn blossom teased my nostrils. As the tranquillity washed over me, my excitement swelled; the true wilds of Dartmoor were within touching distance. Despite the subtle ache nestled between my shoulder blades (and the slightly-less subtle one on my scalp), my earlier doubts about my physical ability were forgotten. Yes – right now I was knackered – but my body would adjust. I was not going to race across Dartmoor. If I needed to stop and rest, I would stop and rest. I had come here to challenge myself – not to kill myself.

With that thought I chomped down the last of my peanut butter sandwich, then set off again.

The path finally stopped climbing and soon after reached the dam, forming a tee-junction with a concrete walkway that crossed the 200-metre-wide, 50-metre-high structure. I strolled out to the centre and stared down at the river that spurted from the north side, then I turned and gazed across the reservoir. Incredibly calm, the surface reflected the pure, unbroken expanse of blue sky above, although this viewpoint offered only a partial view of this body of water, as its curvature through the hills shielded the southern end of the reservoir. Sunlight danced on its surface and somewhere a crow squawked.

Checking the time on my phone, I saw that the four bars indicating the signal strength were no longer lit up. Experiencing something of an epiphany, I switched it off and consigned it to a side-pocket of my pack. From here on, during these long June days and unrestrained by any conventional daily routine, the concept of time would be of minor importance. If and when I might deem that concept necessary again, the clock on my camera would suffice.

That said, somehow my first day had just surpassed 5:00pm, and I still possessed only a vague idea of where I was going to camp. A scan of the surrounding hills ruled out this end of the reservoir. I was also still too close to that picnic area. Spending the night here would *officially* constitute a wild camp – just not quite wild enough.

I left the dam behind and followed the path along the bank of the reservoir, although a thick coppice of small trees and shrubs, protected by a wooden fence, now shielded the water from view. The main path then turned off to the left, heading up an ascent named Longstone Hill. This change in direction corresponded with the route on the map – but the path that continued alongside the reservoir did not.

From that point on, it would be over 24 hours before I would match a path to the map again.

Eager to remain as close to the reservoir as possible, I ignored the path leading up the hill and stuck to my planned (but infinitely vague) route. After a while I reached a footbridge, crossing a narrow stream that flowed through the coppice and into the reservoir. To the left, the stream had gouged out a roughly-triangular, secluded area into the hillside, perhaps 20 metres across and twice as long. A potential camping spot! An exciting one, too; although I'd intended to camp close to the reservoir, I never anticipated being able to pitch my tent just a stone's throw from the shore.

Under the watchful eyes of a few sheep, I followed the brook upstream. Gone was the clumping sound of my boots hitting stony paths or tarmac. Instead my feet dodged sheep-droppings, cowpats, and strips of marshy ground, the latter marked by the tell-tale, dark, spiky plants that I knew thrived on damp ground. My previous rambles had also told me that stepping on one too many of them could result in sodden feet. In the absence of acquainting myself with the name of the species, I referred to them affectionately as the 'Green Hedgehogs' (I may be a nature lover, but I am no nature boffin).

After a few minutes of scouting I came across a flat patch of smooth, bone-dry grass, dipping a foot or two below the surrounding ground, and perfectly sized for my tent. The imposing hills dwarfing either side offered not only privacy, but probably some protection from the wind as well. The blackened remains of a makeshift fireplace indicated that I hadn't been the first to think so. To my dismay, it also contained a few crushed beer cans.

Despite the signs of this being a popular spot, I decided to make camp here for my first night.

I half-sat, half-fell onto a rock and slid my arms from the straps of my pack, then turned around and laid it to rest, unclipping my tent. Like the rest of this hilly alcove, sheep droppings and the odd cowpat littered the ground. Fortunately, most of the latter appeared to be spread just about far enough apart. They had also been deposited some time ago and had crusted over, sparing my nose from any putrid stench. After flicking away the worst of the sheep turds with a stick, my pitch was ready.

I'm no expert when it comes to tents. I've never been one for investing in flashy camping gear with all the bells and whistles. For this trip I'd paid only marginally more consideration to the selection of my home. Crucially the tent needed to be small and lightweight. Other than that, what major considerations were there? I'd paid the modest sum of about forty pounds for this bit of polyester and fibreglass, but following a test-pitching back home, I was confident that it was up to the challenge of housing me for two weeks in the notoriously fickle climate of Dartmoor.

The tent consisted of an inner layer stretched out by a single pole across its width, covered by an outer flysheet. With the whole thing weighing only 2.5 kilogrammes, at least that ticked the most important box. It also weighed a lot less than the tents I normally hauled along on my camping trips. I'd considered an alternative at a mere 1.4 kilogrammes. But that benefit came at a price outside of my budget.

After threading the pole through the inner tent and securing it with the hooks at each end, the tent began to take shape. After repositioning it a few times to avoid the feet-end going on top of a huge cowpat, I grabbed the pegs. I pushed one of them into the earth through a corresponding loop – only for it to hit rock after a few inches. I whacked it with my mallet and it bent like a straw. These were supposed to be heavy-duty rock pegs. I'd had my suspicions about the puny-looking things, but had decided to give them the benefit of the doubt. The same happened with the next peg, so I adopted a gentler approach with the others, resigning myself to the fact that my tent was not going to be pitched as tightly as I would like.

I fixed the flysheet in place over the top, then took my gear inside. Externally, the tent measured about seven feet long and four feet wide. Its limited height forced me to slouch a little inside, but aside from that minor hardship, the living space was sufficient.

Outside I stepped back to admire my home, happily receiving my second shudder of excitement of the day.

Next I needed to replenish my water supply. To minimise my pack weight, I'd decided against a high-capacity hydration pouch, instead favouring a one-litre bottle. This I'd deemed adequate, considering the abundance of blue lines that twisted across my map of Dartmoor. The stream, gurgling away just a few metres from my tent, was inaccessible due to the height and incline of the bank, so I headed back to the footbridge. Along the way I paused frequently, glancing back to assess the discretion of my camp. Although well within my legal rights to camp here, I wanted to be as invisible as possible. To my delight, less than half the tent was visible from about a dozen metres away. By the time I reached the footbridge there was no sign of it whatsoever.

Although easily accessible here, the stream's current was murky and sluggish. I'd brought along purification tablets but was still dubious about drinking water that dribbled through an excrement-filled field.

I trudged back upstream in search of a faster-flowing stretch, eventually finding a small ledge over which the stream formed a mini-waterfall. Getting close to it would involve a nifty leap of about a metre-and-a-half across the water – right onto a clump of the Green Hedgehogs.

I took a short run-up and jumped. On landing, I struggled to gain my balance as the spiky plants squelched beneath my feet. Flapping my arms wildly, I managed to steady myself, then turned around and crouched down to fill my bottle. Tips of the hedgehog-leaves found a gap through my clothes and tickled at my backside.

Following a close examination of the contents, I popped in a chlorine pill. I'd never used such tablets before, and watched with fascination as it fizzed away, leaving a trail of bubbles as it sank to the bottom. I screwed the lid on, turned the bottle upside down, and watched the little fizz-bomb fall again.

I am easily entertained.

After repeating my drunken ballerina impression over the stream, I headed back to the path to explore more of the reservoir's shoreline.

Across the footbridge, the path left the fence, climbing swiftly and leaving a steep, unguarded drop down to the shrubs and trees alongside the reservoir. Once the path reached about 30 metres above the water, the fence returned and the path levelled off. Further along, the flora thinned to reveal an island poking above the water, smothered in thick vegetation. The reservoir snuggled beautifully into the landscape, and had I not passed the dam earlier, I would never have suspected this to be a man-made body of water.

The curve of the reservoir still concealed both its northern and southern tips. Okehampton, too, although only a couple of miles away, was completely obscured by the relatively thin strip of moorland that stretched beyond the water. Had I been blindfolded and dropped in here by helicopter, SAS-style, I could have easily believed I was in the middle of a remote wilderness. Another shudder of excitement gushed through me as I headed back to my camp. Although the notion of me rappelling from a helicopter like an SAS operative was more than slightly ridiculous.

Back near the footbridge, I crossed a stile built into the fence, then weaved my way amongst the trunks of young birch trees to a small pebble beach, where the stream widened and shallowed before trickling into the reservoir. Here I found the remains of another fireplace, in the form of a small circle of blackened stones. Thankfully this one contained no litter.

Glancing up at the sky, I guessed sunset was a little over an hour away. A soft, warm glow was gradually replacing the harsh sunlight that had reflected off the water earlier. The evening would soon be entering what we photographers call the golden hour – a hallowed time of day when the sun hangs low over the horizon, casting a beautiful golden light, interspersed with long shadows, across the landscape. Golden hours had rewarded me with some great shots in recent years. What would those on Dartmoor offer me? As the first one approached, I assessed my opportunities.

To assist with this task, I fished my battered old compass from beneath my tee-shirt. I faced roughly north-west; not a bad direction for a sunset. In the distance, across the reservoir and highlighted by their elongated shadows, cows grazed on the hillside, their bodies little more than specks. A pair of ducks took off, flapping their way across the reservoir a foot or two above the surface, before skidding back onto the water with a maniacal chorus of quacking.

But despite the onset of golden hour, I dismissed any thought of taking photos that evening. As the sun had dipped beneath the hills on the other side of the reservoir, it had become apparent that the day would conclude beneath a cloudless sky – ruling out any epic sunsets. Neither the distant cows nor the ducks offered much inspiration; I could photograph both species to my heart's content within an hour's walk of my flat back home. Neither could I afford to be gratuitous with my shots, since I would have to stretch out my camera's power supply until I could charge my batteries at the campsite, mid-way through my hike. Of far greater appeal was the prospect of capturing a majestic image of tomorrow's sunrise, with fluffy, crimson and orange clouds reflected on the reservoir.

So I headed back to the tent and turned my attention to dinner.

For most of the next 14 days, dinner would consist of a sachet of savoury rice, of which I'd brought a selection of varieties. Lunch would be light: a portion of couscous – specifically, a brand called *Spice Sensation* and endorsed by the huge, grinning face of a celebrity chef on the carton. Breakfast would be satisfied by a flaky, powdery substance – an elementary version of porridge – of which I'd brought along a whopping 1.5kg bagful. A spoonful of sugar, or two, was sufficient to make the stuff palatable. I'd also brought a few chocolate bars and three different sorts of biscuits. Of course, no Englishman's breakfast is complete without a brew, so this necessity was satisfied with a jar of instant white tea, pre-blended with sugar.

I examined my water bottle. The neutraliser – the second of the two pills I'd added – had now fully dissolved. To eliminate water wastage, as part of my hike preparations I'd measured and memorised the exact quantities required to prepare each meal. I poured the amount for a sachet of 'golden vegetable' flavoured rice into my saucepan, then lit the stove.

Whilst waiting for my water to boil, I delicately placed a finger onto the cracked skin of my scalp. Although still tender, a crusty scab had taken the place of that yellow goo. My slight headache would almost certainly be gone by morning, too.

Ten minutes later I was enjoying my first alfresco dinner on Dartmoor.

My pack contained two items reserved for emergency use only. One of them was a 'survival bag' – a thick, orange, waterproof sack, intended to shelter me from the elements in an emergency. This had accompanied me on every camping holiday I'd ever been on – although so far I'd never needed to use it for its intended purpose (I'd once planned to sleep inside it during an astro-photography session, but abandoned that idea after about 30 minutes…).

The other emergency accessory was a flint-and-steel firestarter. Having never used such a thing before, I decided it would be wise to get to grips with it after dinner. Besides, what better way could there be to end my first day than with a cosy campfire by the lakeside? I kept the firestarter in an old tobacco tin, along with some cotton-wool-like material for tinder. After digging it out from my pack, I pulled a few tufts of yellow, bone-dry grass from a nearby tussock, then stomped back down to the fireplace on the beach.

I couldn't help feeling a tad irresponsible as I crossed the stile. Even before my first day had concluded, I was about to break one of the golden rules concerning camping on Dartmoor; open fires were prohibited. But my tiny fire would be lit upon a pebble beach. I wasn't going to be damaging the land whatsoever – unlike those that had used my pitch before me. I would never have dreamt of lighting a fire on the grass, and had I not come across this abandoned fireplace next to the reservoir, the thought wouldn't have even entered my head to light one there, either. A few heavy smatterings of rain would wash away the ashes in due course, so where was the harm? Furthermore, this hike was to be defined by first experiences, and despite my camping experience, I had never bid goodnight in the great outdoors with a real campfire – so my hike should, unquestionably, include one of those, too.

After an eagle-eyed scan of my surroundings to ensure I wasn't being watched, I arranged the cotton wool and grass in the circle of stones. On top of this I placed a few twigs and sticks, with a couple of thicker branches at the ready. I dropped to the ground, groaning as my knees hit the stony beach, then began scraping the steel bar along the flint. After a few strokes I found a rhythm. Almost every strike produced a spark – but the cotton-wool just would not catch it.

I eventually admitted defeat and pulled my lighter from my pocket instead.

Bear Grylls, I am not.

The cotton wool smouldered against the lighter flame then ignited into a tiny fireball. Almost as quickly, the flames whimpered away as the fibres blackened and shrivelled. I delicately blew at the embers, wincing as the gravel further embedded itself into my kneecaps. Moments later my fire flickered into life. The kindling crackled and the timid flames began to dance.

I gingerly placed the larger sticks on top, then sat cross-legged as my fire grew hypnotically. Faint plumes of smoke rose into the air as my eyes wandered across the still, darkening water. Evening shade stretched across most of the reservoir, offering some degree of camouflage to the black plumage of a moorhen scuttling silently across the water, its head bobbing back and forth vigorously, the orange tip of its beak leading the charge. Also silent were the ducks, allowing the crisp, staccato crackle of the fire to punctuate the hushed beauty of the landscape.

This could have been a serene enough ending to my first day, but I wasn't done yet; the sky would quite possibly remain cloudless that night. For me this could mean only one thing: a session of astrophotography beckoned.

I had always been fascinated by astronomy. In fact, my initial reason for buying a DSLR camera had been to photograph the night sky. To me, the stars are the only things that truly reveal just how precious yet insignificant our tiny planet really is amongst the universe. Despite the fact that light travels at an unfathomable 186,282 miles per second, when we observe the stars, they are so distant that we are looking back through time – in some cases, by many thousands of years. We effectively, therefore, become time-travellers – not mere observers. The only thing that tops that concept is photographing the heavenly beauties. To that end, in recent years I'd spent many long nights out in the Worcestershire countryside with my camera, sometimes all night long.

But never in a setting such as this.

Above the wispy trails of smoke, the first stars of the night revealed themselves. At this time of year – close to the summer solstice – total darkness wouldn't arrive until around midnight. But despite the allure of my campfire (although, in truth, the flames were already dying down) I preferred the idea of stepping out later and being dazzled by a vast star-scape, rather than continue to let them creep up on me one by one. So I abandoned my waning fire and strolled back to the tent in the twilight.

I wiled away the next couple of hours flicking between local and national stations on my two-band radio. By torchlight, I also delved into my reader: the autobiography of John Lydon – one of my musical heroes.

At about half-past midnight, equipped with my headlamp, I attached my wide-angle lens and tripod to the camera, then unzipped the tent and stepped out into the darkness.

The chill in the air – on a June night – took me by surprise. My tee-shirt and fleece needed support, so I fumbled through my pack to retrieve my cagoule. Pulling the zip-less jacket over my head, I inadvertently yanked the headlamp down onto my nose with a thump, almost pulling off my glasses. I wriggled my arms into the sleeves, adjusted my facial accessories, then peered up at the sky. As the beam of the headlamp faded into the night air, I gleefully observed how there wasn't even a sliver of cloud overhead.

My spine tingled again as I zipped up the tent.

Picking my way across the rough heathland down toward the bridge, my boots occasionally clashed with the tips of boulders that had evaded the torchlight. Glowing eerily, clusters of tiny white dots hung suspended in mid-air – moments later to be revealed as the eyes of sheep lining the hillside. Despite my encounters with various beasts during my previous photographic exploits after dark, their zombie-like presence was enough to momentarily stop me in my tracks.

The eyes continued to track me as I proceeded to the footbridge. Then, remaining mindful of the steep drop to my right, I headed up the unguarded section of path. Specks of dew danced in the torchlight like ghostly fireflies, mingling with my condensing breath. As soon as the fence returned, I switched the torch to its red beam so as not to hinder the onset of my night vision. Frequently I paused to assess photo opportunities, eventually reaching a clearing through the scrub above the waterline. The huge, grey form of the reservoir began to emerge through the darkness.

This was what I had been searching for.

My fingers found the rubber rings that unlocked each section of the tripod's legs. I extended it to its maximum height, switched off the headlamp, then waited for my eyes to fully accustom to the dark, gradually teasing out whatever details I could of the landscape.

Soon enough, a shimmering reflection of starlight replaced the dull form of the reservoir. Beyond, the treeline of the opposite shore formed a band of spiky blackness, stabbing at the faint glow on the horizon, where the streetlights of Okehampton attempted to infiltrate the night. Suddenly something dunked beneath the water. The smooth surface rippled out in circles, directing the starlight in an intimate dance.

Then silence engulfed me once more.

I traced the constellations of Cygnus and Cassiopeia. There were many more, of course, but I was better acquainted with the winter constellations. Also discernible was the faint outline of the Milky Way, stretching diagonally across the sky, mimicking the ghostly residue of some giant aquatic creature, frozen in time whilst leaping from the water.

I set to work with my camera. My gear wasn't perfect for astro-photography by a long way. The cool air repeatedly condensed on the lens, too, forcing me to reach for the wad of scrunched-up toilet paper in my pocket. Ordinarily I would have fixed a few heat pads around the lens. But they were another of those last-minute, convenient-but-non-essential items that I'd ditched whilst packing. Another impediment was light pollution from the town – barely visible to the naked eye, but much more apparent on my long-exposure photographs. But after half a dozen or so attempts, I managed to capture something satisfying.

On my way back to the tent I took a few shots from the beach.

Whilst waiting for one of my 30-second exposures to conclude, I scraped at the remains of my fire with a stick, resuscitating a few tiny embers into a pulsating glow. As I reviewed my final shot of the night, they glowed no more.

Soon after that I crawled back into my sleeping bag – still as exhilarated as the moment I'd crawled out of it.

But now I needed sleep. Tomorrow my hike would *really* begin – higher and deeper into the moor. The aches in my back and my head were gone. But the rest of my body was beaten. And yet, as physically shattered as I was, and although the clock on my camera displayed 01:42, my mind refused to switch off.

Even if I had been able to get my body and mind to sync, the breeze was no longer a gentle one. I had assumed earlier that the steep hills either side of my camp would offer some protection from the wind. That assumption was wrong, and the inconsiderate night air was now thumping at my less-than-perfectly-pegged tent.

I reviewed my shots again, then lay still in the darkness, trying to ignore the pounding wind...trying to expel from my mind the events of that first day...and the anticipation of the days to come.

But to no avail. All through my first night on Dartmoor, I didn't sleep for a single minute.

Chapter Two: Paths

Meldon Reservoir to Brat Tor

One obvious benefit to a sleepless night was the assurance that I would be awake in time for a dawn photography session. However, when I poked my head outside the tent at about 4:30am, the twilight sky was devoid of even a wisp of cloud. That photo I'd envisaged was to be consigned to my imagination; there would be no pretty reflections on the reservoir that morning.

That realisation was sufficient to persuade me to zip up the tent and snuggle back into my sleeping bag, as the dawn chorus of birdsong – with strong competition from the wind – narrated the seamless passage of time as I drifted wearily into day two of my hike.

A rather dismissive attitude for a photographer, I know. Amongst the key attributes required for this hobby are adaptability and the willingness to abandon expectations. However, at that time I was still pretty much a newcomer to the hobby; I was yet to fully appreciate such disciplines. But more accountable for my abstinence, right there and then, was the simple fact that I was knackered. I told myself that – considering the events of yesterday, followed by zero hours' kip – a little laziness was justified.

About an hour later I talked myself into going for a wander. Having slept in both my tee-shirt and my fleece, I expected to remove the latter on stepping outside, only to discover my private little campsite had yet to escape the cooling shadow of the hills.

Remaining double-layered, I strolled down to the reservoir. My legs required a little more heave than expected to cross the stile – but cross they did, and I tottered through the trees down to the beach.

A couple of blackened sticks poked out from the deathly-grey remains of my campfire. After a cautious temperature-check, I tossed the stones into the bushes, then scuffed a boot across the pebbles to disperse the incriminating, powdery flakes – fully satisfied that following a good downpour, no-one but Columbo would find any evidence of my crime.

I hopped across the stream where it met the reservoir, then followed the shoreline along the dozen metres or so that the trees would permit. Crouching down, I sunk my palms into the water, allowing them to rest on the gravelly bed. My fingers scrunched through the gravel, turning the water opaque with brown sediment. As the cold water began to bite, I withdrew my hands and something splashed in the water nearby, sending ripples out across the water.

A thin ribbon of mist clung to the reservoir's opposite shore. The morning haze had veiled the hills beyond; their texture now matched the pale sky overhead. I considered going back for my camera. Since arriving here I'd been imagining an epic, technicolour sunrise shot over this body of water – but this scene was just as worthy of a space on the memory card. As a self-proclaimed photography addict, what was I thinking, coming down here without my camera, turning my nose up at a wonderful photo opportunity?

But a significant factor in the beauty of this scene was the fact that in a matter of minutes, this view, in its current form, would be gone. The sun would breach the hills behind me, burning away the mist and bathing the opposing ridge in golden sunlight. This made the moment all the more precious. Sure, I could run back and grab my camera and be back in five minutes, probably still in time to snap the last of the mist – or maybe not. Either way, that would be five minutes of this moment lost.

How many other such moments would there be on this hike? Moments not meant to be shared. Certainly not in the form of a photograph, at least. A few such moments would be not only desirable – but an essential component of my time on Dartmoor. Moments not pre-conceived, but rather that I'd arrived at purely by circumstance. This moment was borne of my simply wandering down here without any thought of taking pictures – and that was how the moment should conclude.

So, there I remained until the last of the mist had departed. The long shadows of the hillside followed as the sun crept higher behind me, its invigorating glow sweeping over the trees along the opposite shore.

My first Dartmoor dawn was over.

As I was climbing back over the stile I caught sight of a red, furry creature scampering across the hilly alcove. Its nimble legs, driving much darker, almost black feet, negotiated the hillside effortlessly. It was, unmistakably, a fox. Suddenly the animal paused and turned to face me, its vulpine ears pricked. For a second or two, a pair of dark, accusatory eyes met mine, then returned to evasive mode before disappearing over the top of the hill.

Perhaps he'd picked up the scent of my food, and had kindly popped down here to relieve me of some of that heavy load? I would have been only mildly surprised to see him brazenly sauntering away with sachets of my rice between his teeth. But there was no sign of any intrusion at the tent. Perhaps I wasn't carrying his preferred brand?

As I waited for the sun to lift the morning dew from the flysheet, I prepared breakfast, setting up my stove inside the tent to escape the breeze. I also wanted to re-hydrate some couscous for a ready-prepared lunch.

Once the water reached a vigorous boil I brewed a cup of tea, then tossed a massive handful of the powdery porridge flakes into the pan – only for half of the stuff to be blown back all over me. I screwed up my face and snorted, then scowled as I glanced down at my oat-speckled sleeping bag.

In future I would prepare my breakfast with the tent fully zipped up.

Before any residue of porridge could weld itself to my saucepan, I washed up at the same spot where I'd filled my bottle. Soon after – and following a thorough shakeout of my sleeping bag – I was fully packed. But despite having scoffed down a hearty portion of porridge and half a dozen custard creams with my tea, I felt quite lethargic – slightly faint, even. Something of an inevitability after last night's sleep deprivation, I supposed.

Despite my level of anticipation, I wasn't quite ready to move on just yet – and my lethargy wasn't the only reason. In recent years I'd become accustomed to a pretty regular bowel movement. To be precise, by 10:00am on most days I would have shed a few pounds. Less certain but still quite common was more shedding in the early afternoon. Such was my regularity that this had even been observed by former colleagues, and running jokes had ensued in regard to my '9:30 appointments'. I'd therefore expected to pay a visit to a train-toilet on my journey down to Devon. That hadn't happened. In fact, there had been no stirrings at all throughout that first day. Surely things were about to change...?

I possessed no qualms about doing the deed in the outdoors, and my little camp here was perfectly suited. Not only for its discreet location, but it even came with a handy tree from which I could hang onto whilst leaning back to drop my cargo. Who knew if I would find such ideal amenities later in the day? It made sense, therefore, to hang around and see if I could erase this distraction before setting off.

Whilst waiting for any excretal stirrings, I spread the map out over the patch of grass that my groundsheet had just vacated, and reviewed my intended route for the day ahead. I would first head for the southern end of the reservoir (assuming the shoreline path went that far). From there, with hardly any marked paths covering the next few miles, my exact route was unclear, but I would continue south, climbing up towards Corn Ridge and then on to Great Links Tor. Time permitting, Brat Tor would mark my second camp, roughly a mile-and-a-half south-west of Great Links Tor.

After half an hour my hopes of shedding a modicum of weight before setting off had faded. I couldn't hang around any longer; I would just have to take my chances.

Just as I was about to set off, three soldiers, fully kitted out in camouflage gear and carrying backpacks and rifles, crossed the footbridge at a brisk pace. Within five minutes a whole platoon had passed, followed by two middle-aged civilians, hot on their heels and dressed in expensive-looking hiking gear, carrying small daypacks and walking poles.

The sight of this military procession was no huge surprise; large parts of Dartmoor, the north-west in particular, are used as a training ground by the British Forces. The largest of these three military ranges is the Okehampton Range, the border of which lay about a mile to the east – presumably where the platoon was heading.

This was my first sighting of any humans since leaving that picnic area yesterday. I felt a vague sense of intrusion as they passed, although none of them spotted me as I spied on them from my vacated pitch (and redundant toilet). They were all moving in the same direction as I would be heading, so I lingered for a while to let them get ahead. If I was going to keel over from exhaustion (or need to take a crap), the last thing I wanted was an audience.

Once confident that they were all well ahead, I dragged my pack up onto the rock near my pitch and slipped into the straps. Then, using the tree trunk, I hauled myself to my feet.

My lethargy left me soon after I got moving, and after passing last night's stargazing location the path gently descended and I picked up the pace, keen to maximise my progress during this easy stage of the day's route. Somewhere, a mile or two up ahead, amongst the hills, Corn Ridge awaited me. I fully expected the terrain to toughen as I headed deeper and higher into the moor – but despite my lack of sleep my confidence had grown. A little, at least.

I soon caught up with the two walkers I'd spied on earlier, forcing me to slow down. On a day shaping up to be just as warm as the preceding one, both were wearing full waterproofs and gaiters. Surely a little over-cautious…? Then again, what did I know as to what constituted appropriate Dartmoor clothing? I was a novice moorland hiker – and a stranger to these parts. These two were probably locals. If we took the same route over the next two weeks, I wouldn't be at all surprised if they beat me to Ivybridge, despite my relative youth. I would stagger into town, filthy and delirious with exhaustion, to find them sat leisurely outside a café, enjoying a Devon cream tea with smug grins etched upon their faces – and not so much as a speck of mud on their gaiters.

I hung back, listening to the clicking of their walking poles, waiting for an opportunity to overtake them on the narrow path. They'd appeared not to sense my presence. Then they came to a sudden halt, turning to face me.

'If you want to get in front, you won't get far, there's a platoon of soldiers up ahead,' the one directly in front of me said, perhaps a little abruptly as she stepped aside to let me pass. Her companion silently followed suit.

'Yeah, I know…thanks,' was all I could offer in reply as I passed. Had my eagerness to overtake them caused offense? I certainly hadn't intended any. Wasting little thought on the matter, I offered a conciliatory smile then carried on, gradually leaving them behind.

Soon the reservoir became a river again, crossed by a narrow footbridge. On the other side the path opened out onto a patch of flat, rocky pasture. The shallow, swiftly flowing river veered off to the left and another stream fed into the reservoir to the right, crossed by a picturesque stone bridge. A sign marked the land on the other side of the stream as private property, and from the bridge a track passed along the bottom of a steep wooded hill before disappearing along the other side of the reservoir.

The flat pasture extended for a couple of hundred metres before succumbing to a steep climb – which the soldiers were now ascending, setting a somewhat more laboured pace than earlier (though still far quicker than I expected to manage when my turn came to negotiate that hill). I watched their silhouettes reach the top and disappear over the ridge, then decided it would be sensible to take a break before starting the climb myself.

I removed my pack and perched on the bough of a fallen tree, admiring a beautiful hawthorn in full blossom on the stream's opposite bank. Minutes later the two gaiter-clad walkers crossed the footbridge, before following the path along the river and disappearing amongst the curve of its banks.

Whilst also observing the route of the West Okemont River, my attention alternated between the map and the rock formation at the top of a hill to the east. I deduced that those rocks must be Black Tor. I was eager to get up close to my first tor – of which there are over 160 on Dartmoor. However, adding this one to my itinerary would add an extra mile or two, as presumably I would have to come back this way to cross the river, in the absence of any bridge marked on the map further upstream.

I told myself I should stick to my planned route – at least until I'd broken myself in. I also needed to bear in mind that on occasion my knees struggled with steep-gradient walking (such discomfort had sometimes befallen me whilst descending The Malverns and Bredon Hill – my most frequented walking locations near to home).

I set off again, crossing another footbridge over the river to take the same route up the hill as the soldiers. At the start of the climb I paused, rather pointlessly, to assess the gradient for a final time. Then up I went.

Up. And up. And up. Fighting against gravity, I hunched forward to balance the weight of my pack against the incline. My leg muscles engaged alternately with everything they had, like the pistons of a clapped-out car, chugging up a steep lane. The path pushed back just as hard and my feet skidded once or twice on the gravelly surface. Every few minutes I paused for breath, leaning forward with my hands on my knees, facing the dirt, fighting the temptation to look up as my heart pounded against my chest. At one point I almost gave in, standing upright and momentarily sacrificing my centre of balance. With a split-second to spare I recovered my diminutive stature and willed myself on before the hill could claim me. After an eternity the gradient suddenly levelled off.

Finally I could stand upright again, and as I did so the path took a sharp bend to the left – then disappeared. I glanced around, expecting to see the soldiers somewhere in the distance.

There was no-one in sight.

I virtually collapsed onto the stony earth and crawled out of my pack, wiping my forehead with my hat. A few beads of sweat managed to evade my mopping action, trickling down the side of my face. I took a few swigs of water. I wanted to drink more – a lot more – but I had no idea when I would next be able to fill my bottle. I could have topped up at the river, of course, but that would have meant possibly contaminating my purified water. And if I popped in another pill on top of those I'd added earlier, would I be overdosing on my chlorine consumption…?

My mind drifted back to my brother's reaction when I'd told him of my plans. He would have loved to have seen me like this. I imagined him standing over me with his trademark smirk. A smirk I knew only too well – the one he could never contain whenever we discussed my participation in any physical activity.

Although only three years my senior, he had always been the fitter and sportier of the two of us, going right back to our teens. I remember once challenging him to a race around the athletics track on the school playing fields. Somewhere on the second lap I'd collapsed in submission – whilst he'd barely broken a sweat. I never dared to challenge him again.

His physical prowess over me was no stroke of luck, though. He hadn't been awarded preferential treatment from our gene pool, but had exercised regularly ever since the onset of that peculiar phase of life we call puberty. I, on the other hand, was always the kid picked last for football team selection when we lined up against the wall in P.E.. That was fair enough, though; I *was* useless on the pitch. Rugby was even worse. I wasn't merely indifferent – I hated it. All that grabbing and shoving and ear-chewing. So rather than subject myself to inevitable mockery, I'd sometimes volunteer a gang of us for a cross-country run instead, preferring a gentle jog around the nearby woods (or a game of 'man-hunt' – a staple activity for any adolescent boy in 1990s Britain. Probably now banned in schools for 'Health & Safety' reasons).

Those inescapable P.E. lessons aside, I avoided physical activity whenever possible throughout childhood. Little changed after reaching adulthood. Except for a period of my late twenties, when something odd came over me (a delayed conclusion of puberty, perhaps?) that prompted me to take up squash. Two or three years of racquet-breaking was enough of that. But despite my apathy towards any conscious form of exercise, and the sizeable gut I've sported for half of my adult life, I've always managed to maintain a decent level of stamina – probably thanks in no small part to the considerable amount of walking I do. But on Dartmoor, was I expecting a little too much of myself…?

My brother still reigns supreme over our family in the fitness stakes, and now teaches the martial art of Muay Thai. He has, now and again, tried to rouse some inclination in me to have a go at it. Only once have I ever given in to his persuasions, indulging him with a sparring session. However, as he savagely pummelled the pads strapped to my arms and legs, almost sending me flying across the room, he finally realised this was a sport that would fare better *without* my participation.

He never extended such an invitation again.

My heart and lungs slowly recovered from that climb…then I took out the map and compass again. After studying some nearby field boundaries, I pinpointed my location with reasonable accuracy. I also managed to discern the resumption of the path, heading in the direction of a distant rock formation named as Sourton Tors. But

Corn Ridge was about 90-degrees to the left of this direction. Assuming I'd read the map correctly, on the way to Corn Ridge I would come across another large rock formation – Branscombe's Loaf – only about half a mile away. Yet despite the gradient having now eased considerably, those rocks were nowhere to be seen.

I climbed back into my pack and heaved myself onto all fours, then staggered to my feet. I took a final glance around. Ignoring that vague path, I set off in the direction that would hopefully lead me to Branscombe's Loaf.

A clump of boulders soon poked up across my eyeline. The terrain became rockier as they drew closer, until the grass was all but gone, with many of the boulders now as big as my pack. Was this Branscombe's Loaf? I hoped not; these rocks were pretty unremarkable. Unworthy of noting on a map, anyway. But even though by this point I'd squeezed the map conveniently into the side-pocket of my trousers, I refused to take it out again a mere ten minutes or so since my last map-check.

On I went across a patchwork of green and grey as the rocks thinned. The breeze increased with my elevation, and after pausing to document this location on my camcorder, I reviewed the footage only to find my voice lost amongst the roar of wind distortion on the microphone.

As I watched the image on the screen pan around, the video clip revealed the extent of the moors in almost every direction. No more than a kilometre ahead, Corn Ridge rose above the rocky plain, rolling from north to south as far as the eye could see. Close to the northern end, the rocks of Sourton Tors were still visible. To the east, the moor dived briefly into that punishingly-steep valley of the West Okemont River before stretching ever onward. Only a thin slice of land, far away on the eastern horizon, reflected a more conventional English countryside: a few tame, flat fields, bordered by trees and hedgerows. An infinitely mundane landscape in comparison to what faced me in every other direction.

I pushed on, and minutes later more grey boulders crept into view – much larger and more distinctive then the previous batch.

Soon I was almost amongst them. I removed my pack and set it between two of the hundreds – if not thousands – of smaller rocks surrounding this feature. A feature that certainly *was* worthy of naming on a map. With not a soul around, I felt confident enough to leave my pack unattended, so after extracting my camera gear I weaved through the boulders to greet Branscombe's Loaf.

These rocks were named after Walter Branscombe – a Bishop of Exeter in the thirteenth century. As legend has it, one misty evening, whilst riding across the moor with his chaplain, he was stopped by a man offering him bread and cheese. As the bishop was about to take a bite, the chaplain noticed that sticking out from beneath the stranger's cloak were hooves instead of feet. He therefore deduced that the stranger was, in fact, the Devil. Anyone who ate food from the hand of Satan would be forever under his command. Naturally. Rushing to the bishop's aid, the chaplain dashed the bread and cheese to the ground, where they transformed into boulders, and the thwarted Devil disappeared.

Myself, I favoured the geological theory of how this feature, along with most of Dartmoor, was created: the granite upon which approximately 65 percent of Dartmoor sits was formed some 300 million years ago. Around 50 million years ago, the land mass we now know as Devon was a much hotter and humid place than today, and acidic water eroded and shaped the granite into early forms of the tors. Over the past two million years, Britain's climate has alternated between temperate and sub-arctic, and alternate freezing and thawing has cracked and split the rock, creating boulder fields, whilst the elements have carved the tips of the very hardest granite into the unique tors this slab of England is now famed for.

I couldn't admit to identifying anything resembling a loaf of bread or a lump of cheese as I approached the boulders…but what peculiar wonders they were, in some cases appearing to defy gravity. Others looked as if a crane had meticulously assembled them into works of modern art. Something of an illusion, though, the nature of their formation had dictated their haphazard appearance; the huge cracks that appeared to split the rocks were formed as the granite cooled and contracted, so despite their appearing to consist of numerous boulders all having been piled on top of each other, this was, by enlarge, not the case.

Up close, I studied the collage of lichens that covered the rocks. There are up to 60 species of this resilient little organism found on Dartmoor – including some varieties that are commonly found in the arctic.

Inserting my hand into one of those 300 million-year-old, lichen-filled cracks in the rock, my fingers met something coarse and bone-dry, like the desiccated, shed skin of a rattlesnake.

At the edge of Branscombe's Loaf I observed the steep valley dropping to the east, along with a patch of stunted, gnarly little oak trees nestled into the other hillside, perhaps a kilometre away. The map identified this feature as Black-a-Tor Copse, one of Dartmoor's three ancient woodlands. High above the trees perched Black Tor, the rocks I'd noted before following those soldiers up the hill.

(The soldiers – where had they gone???).

By my reckoning, I'd completed about a third of the day's route – but hadn't really covered that much distance. I wondered how many hours of daylight remained. That concept – time – that I'd flippantly dismissed the previous afternoon suddenly became important again. But according to my camera it was only about 2:00pm. I had plenty of time to reach my camping location near Brat Tor.

I headed back to my pack and dug out the tub of couscous I'd prepared that morning. Spice 'Sensation' seemed a generous name for the stuff. But regardless of the taste, my appetite had deserted me. After forcing down a few mouthfuls with my plastic spork – just for the sake of my energy levels – I set off again in my quest to reach Corn Ridge.

The rocky surface gradually gave way to softer, mushier terrain, forcing me into a winding route up the hill. Frequently I paused to catch my breath, whilst glancing back at Branscombe's Loaf to gauge my progress. As the crow flies, the highest point of Corn Ridge lay no more than half a kilometre from Branscombe's Loaf – a fact I repeatedly reminded myself of as I panted away. If my map-checks were correct, and providing I maintained a south-westerly direction, once I reached the very top, Great Links Tor would reveal itself. The terrain would then be reasonably flat, with the hard work over for that day.

Then, out of nowhere, a young couple appeared a short distance away, laughing and smiling and swinging their linked hands. The girl, wearing a flowery summer dress, repeatedly brushed her long blonde hair from her eyes as it swished in the wind. Her darker-haired lover wore a short-sleeved shirt and denim shorts, displaying his muscular limbs to great effect. It was the most romantic scene that I'd witnessed in quite some time – with the possible exception being that of a pair of courting puffins I'd seen once on a David Attenborough programme. At the same time, though, as intriguing and absorbing as I was finding Dartmoor, describing the place as romantic was proving a little challenging.

So engrossed were they with each other, there was little chance that the pair had seen me. But that was enough voyeurism for one day. I turned my attention back to my search for Great Links Tor.

The sighting of the young lovers led me to suspect that an unmarked path crossed the ridge. Or, at least, that the ground was much firmer higher up, judging by the ease with which they strolled along, devoting far more of their attention to each other's eyes than to their footing. They vanished over the ridge after a few minutes but reappeared intermittently as the climb began to level off.

Eventually I reached almost flat ground. Then, to my right, in the mid-distance, I spotted a trig point; the marker that confirmed the highest point of this hill – 537 metres above sea level.

Not exactly Everest. But I was shattered.

The grass, although now much drier, still couldn't be described as firm. The rocks had gone, but in their place, thick spongy grasses formed huge tussocks a few feet apart. Again, in nearly every direction the moor stretched on to infinity. Only now it resembled a featureless wilderness. No rock formations. No valleys. No rivers or streams. No trees or bushes. No lovers walking hand-in-hand. Just a thick, undulating shagpile of green and yellow.

Neither was there any sign of Great Links Tor…still. It should have surely popped up somewhere by this point? At 586 metres it was roughly 50 metres higher than the trig point not far from where I stood. Then I reminded myself that although close to that marker, I wasn't quite at that elevation *here*. I told myself the tor would appear soon enough. I also told myself I'd earned another rest.

In the absence of any rocks, I crouched down and let my pack pull me down onto one of the tussocks. My backside had barely hit the thick grass when my pack then decided to fall over, taking me with it. I heaved the thing back upright with my shoulders, then slid out of the straps and laid it to rest.

The grass towered over me as I slouched on the ground. I'd read that a healthy population of adders had made Dartmoor their home. Was it sensible to be sitting here? I dismissed the thought as ridiculous. This was England. People do NOT get bitten by poisonous snakes in England…right? Besides, I'd heard the same thing said about adders on the Malvern Hills – and the most dangerous creature I'd ever encountered up there was an excitable Yorkshire Terrier, who'd taken a little too keen an interest in my breakfast doughnuts.

Whilst forcing down another few mouthfuls of couscous, I noticed the pink hue developing on my forearms. Due to its altitude, Dartmoor is exposed to the south-westerly airflow of the Mid-Atlantic drift. As warm air is forced up over the high ground, it cools, creating generally cloudier conditions, lower temperatures, and more rainfall than lowland areas.

That's what the internet tells you anyway, and I'd become convinced that Dartmoor would greet me with a climate sympathetic towards hikers. Sun cream, therefore, was an item I could dispense with to save a bit of weight. A whole 100 grams of it.

On the plus side, the notion that I was still only a few hours' walk from any urban environment was long gone. Finally, I had reached the true wilds of Dartmoor. I had waited for that realisation since stepping off the bus – but for some reason the expected shudder of excitement never came.

I got to my feet and stared ahead at the beautifully bleak landscape, unable to quell the notion that I should perhaps turn back and find a path. But doing so would add considerable time and distance to my route, so I set off still on that same compass bearing, telling myself that once I clapped eyes on the tor I could just head straight towards it.

But soon I was to realise that this landscape presented challenges other than steep gradients. Yes – I was now on a reasonably flat, open plain, but the knee-high grass now entangled my feet with every step. The tussocks grew larger and the gaps between them smaller. Negotiating them was like walking across a load of old mattresses. Over the years I'd spent countless hours trekking off the beaten track, up and down hills and mountains; through undergrowth; woods; fields of crops.

Now *grass* was getting the better of me.

The seeds of my error had been sown whilst deciding on my route; I'd always planned to cut across the top of Corn Ridge – despite the fact that as well as featuring not a single path across its highest point, the whole area was designated as bracken, heath or rough grassland on the map. Awesome decision, Marky Boy!

Suddenly a cluster of rocks popped up on the horizon. Great Links Tor, surely…?

Their position relative to the map and compass was about perfect. I was just slightly confused as to their distance. Whilst seeming reasonably close, nothing accompanied them to offer any sense of scale. But close or not, remaining on this trajectory would mean slow progress in reaching them.

According to the map, a track lay just under a mile to the west of where I stood – a track leading to within a few hundred metres of Great Links Tor. But locating it would involve a detour of about 90-degrees to the right and walking straight towards...nothing. I had no idea how well-defined this track was. It was entirely possible that it would be just as inconspicuous as the path that had disappeared after that steep climb earlier on. Crucially, though, assuming I *could* find it, it would add another mile, or two, to my route. But those miles would almost certainly be easier than what faced me here.

But did I want to do everything the easy way? Whilst I hadn't come to Dartmoor under the pretence that I was undertaking some epic journey of self-discovery...to push myself to the limit...blah, blah, blah...I still wanted a *bit* of an adventure. Had I really spent weeks breaking in a new pair of hiking boots just to stroll daintily along Dartmoor's dusty paths? I think not!

That settled it. I was sticking to my route. Besides, the only major obstacle would be a stream just up ahead. This sprung from a nearby well, so on reaching it I would simply head upstream and cross it at the source. A dark green stripe sliced across the moor in the mid-distance – most likely vegetation lining the stream in question.

Encouraged, a little, I plodded on. But as that green stripe drew nearer, the earth began to soften again and my boots squelched as they disappeared into those crevices between the tussocks.

Then came the midges. And guess what other toiletry had been dispensed with to save a piddly bit of weight. That's right: insect repellent. I was well aware of how bothersome midges could be in certain areas of the UK – particularly in Scotland. For reasons still not quite clear to me, though, I'd gotten it into my head that midges were not prevalent in southern England.

Although tolerable whilst on the move, each time I paused for breath they swarmed at me, undeterred by my swiping. What a rare feast my pink flesh must have been; had any other human being ever even set foot upon this wild stretch of moorland?

A long, wide, strip of mud.

That was what the 'stream' amounted to. Dozens of the Green Hedgehogs sprouted across it. I scanned over the terrain 'upstream', seeking out the well named as Lyd Head on the map. All I saw was more of the same.

I grabbed a stick and pushed it into the mud, reaching the bottom after a couple of feet. By comparison, the hedgehogs seemed to be supported by relatively firm earth. Could I use them as stepping-stones?

My boots were beginning to sink into the green mush. Flies and midges buzzed around my head. I racked my brain for another option. There wasn't one. Not really. Again I considered that supposed path to the west...but the odds of my finding it were unchanged.

I picked out somewhere to cross, where the mud stretched about 15 feet wide and only a foot or so deep at the edge. There were narrower sections, but here the hedgehogs were spread only a foot or so apart. Whether or not they would take the combined weight of my pack and myself was another matter.

I poked the nearest, decent-sized stump with my stick, testing for firmness, then stepped onto it. The residing hedgehog squirmed beneath my boots. Then the stump began to crumble at the edges. I quickly transferred a foot onto another. Leaning forward so as not to over-balance, and using my stick for support, the other foot followed. This hedgehog reacted much like its neighbour. I crossed to another stump, continuing in this method and changing course wherever necessary. After seven or eight stumps, terra firma lay just a few steps away.

I gave the mud a final depth-test. My stick sank by only a few inches. I stepped across and my left foot sank by about six inches. The right foot followed but hit firmer ground than its partner, almost throwing me off balance. I lunged forward, heaving my feet out of the gunge. With each stride, the mud sucked at my boots with a rowdy fart. After a few metres I reached solid ground, with my boots each resembling a squashed chocolate gateau. With a triumphant smile, I turned to examine my route across the bog.

I flung my stick into the mud and got moving again.

Following that crossing, the rocks that I believed to be Great Links Tor alternately disappeared and re-appeared as the moorland undulated across my south-westerly compass bearing. Along my route I passed an insignificant clump of rocks named Hunt Tor. According to the map I also crossed a track somewhere close by – but could find no evidence of this amongst the terrain. About an hour after passing that tor I reached the top of a subtle elevation named Woodcock Hill, where suddenly Great Links Tor leapt out before me – now less than a kilometre away.

For the second time in less than an hour, I smiled…

There could no longer be any doubt as to the identity of these rocks. For one thing, the presence of sheep grazing at their base finally gave the landmark a sense of scale. The whole formation was perhaps 150 metres across and, including the modest hill upon which it sat, about half as high. Quite different to Branscombe's Loaf, these rocks resembled piles of gigantic, thick, bluey-grey cookies and pancakes, stacked on top of each other and waiting to be drizzled in maple syrup – although in light of my current provisions I failed to appreciate this reminder of such culinary treats.

From there on, the terrain altered significantly. The spongy grasses were replaced by spiny bushes of yellow-flowered gorse, upon a much grittier landscape. Shallow pits and craggy trenches scarred the stony earth, often in sets of vaguely parallel lines. I could have been walking across the scabby carcass of some gigantic, otherworldly beast, its skin having been shredded by the claws of an even more gargantuan predator. A slightly earthlier explanation for the terrain lay within its history; this area had been extensively mined for both peat and tin during Dartmoor's industrial past.

The view of the tor from here was worthy of a photograph. I

would have even tolerated the midges for such a purpose – but there was nowhere flat or stable enough for me to remove my pack and get out my camera gear. So, on I battled, clambering in and out of the pits and trenches as they demanded.

I progressed to within a few hundred metres of the rocks, then the ground dropped into a smooth, shallow trench, about the width of a country lane. A track. A track that, according to the map, crossed the boggy stream about a mile back. Probably the same track that I may well have come across if I'd made that 90-degree turn before negotiating my route across the mud.

I debated whether to abandon the tough terrain in favour of the track, which although didn't lead right up to the tor, would eliminate the last of this rugged landscape before reaching the short climb up to the rocks. But the idea of taking any path now, so near to the end of my mammoth crossing of Corn Ridge, just seemed wrong.

I would finish as I had started.

Throwing myself upon the mercy of Great Links Tor, I let my pack pull me to the floor, then dragged myself from the straps and stretched out on the smooth grass that carpeted the earth around the rocks. The late-afternoon sunshine was waning, exposing the prickly heat radiating from my sunburnt, midge-ravaged skin. The breeze alleviated those symptoms somewhat, and, combined with the bone-dry ground, had designated this hilltop a midge-free zone.

I stared across my route intently, attempting to trace the path I'd taken from Corn Ridge. It was an ambitious expectation, and after a minute or two of scanning the infinite collage of browns, yellows and greens, I admitted defeat.

Although not at the top of any massive hill, my elevation was just shy of 586 metres above sea level – confirmed by the trig point towering behind me on top of the tor. I'd read that on a clear day it was possible to see all the way to Cornwall from here. But despite the glorious weather, a thin haze had descended on the horizon, restricting the view westwards to no more than perhaps 15 miles beyond the nearby parish of Bridstowe, where the moors gave way to farmland at the edge of the national park. Amicombe Hill lay to the east, a little over a mile away. Beyond, the moor would stretch on for many, many miles.

I followed the curve of that track across the landscape as it curled around Great Links Tor before disappearing. Had I found that route earlier it would have shaved off over half of that tough terrain. But as I chipped at the crusts of dried mud on my trousers, I told myself I'd taken the adventurous route. Then, whilst studying the map, a ridiculous realisation swelled up inside my sun-baked brain: the highest point of Corn Ridge, as the crow flies, was just short of a mile-and-a-half from Great Links Tor.

It had taken me two-and-a-half hours to walk a mile-and-a-half.

What made this so difficult to comprehend was that I walked a lot. I walked everywhere. I walked *fast*. Outside of a dodgems ride on a fairground, I've never sat behind a steering wheel in my life – other than for my one unofficial driving lesson, aged 19, in my then-girlfriend's car, around a deserted industrial estate on a Sunday afternoon (apparently my steering was okay, but my pedal control left a lot to be desired). That was purely to satisfy my curiosity – I've never possessed any real desire to learn to drive. Neither was I a frequent user of public transport, my philosophy being that if a journey was walkable in under an hour, then paying for a ride was unnecessary. Lazy, even.

Anyway, I once timed myself walking along a stretch of my local canal. From one mile-marker to another took 16 minutes. A mile in 16 minutes...to this!

But this was no canal towpath. Neither did I carry an 85-litre backpack to work. A part of me felt a tad embarrassed at my progress that afternoon. But it was a small part. Tiny, in fact. I put those thoughts to bed and got up to explore Great Links Tor.

Carrying nothing but my camera gear, I strolled leisurely amongst the massive boulders. Other than the soft plodding of my boots on the grass, only two sounds broke the silence. The first (and the dominant of the two) was the whistling of wind through the rocks. This also persuaded me to put on my long-sleeved shirt, which had remained tied around my waist since leaving Meldon Reservoir. The second, and slightly less ethereal but equally as welcoming sound, was the occasional bleating of sheep. Along with the obligatory droppings, clumps of their matted wool decorated the base of the rocks.

In a small enclave at the eastern end of the tor, crudely buried beneath a few stones, I spotted a scrunched-up wad of toilet paper. I had a good idea of what lay beneath it: droppings of a different kind. Although I hadn't seen another human being since the couple on Corn Ridge, this discovery dented my sense of isolation a little. It also reminded me of the fact that over 48 hours had passed since I'd last emptied my bowels – a fact I was just as puzzled by as I was grateful for. Finding myself caught short on the open expanse of Corn Ridge could have proven rather undignified...

I climbed up to the trig marker near the opposite end of the rocks, which officially declared the aforementioned altitude of 586 metres – although this isn't quite the highest point on Dartmoor. That accolade belongs to a hill known as High Willhays, at 621 metres. This location also happens to be the highest point of the UK, south of the Brecon Beacons in Wales. Hot on its heels is Yes Tor, about a kilometre to the north of its neighbour, at 619 metres. These locations lay just a couple of miles north-west of where I stood. In fact, I'd passed even closer to Yes Tor during my stay at Meldon Reservoir. However, both were situated within the boundary of the Okehampton Firing Range, therefore access to these areas would be off limits until the following day (Saturday) – by which point I would be heading further south.

The first kilometre or so beyond Great Links Tor consisted of more of the stony, bracken and gorse-covered, brown scab I'd negotiated earlier. Beyond, the undulating moorland hills, capped here and there by more tors, stretched on to infinity. Upon one of the clumps of rocks that besieged Great Links Tor, a solitary sheep stood motionless. The curved horns protruding from the head of the beast indicated it was a ram. Although too distant for me to perceive any eyes amongst his black, anonymous face, I was certain his glare was fixed on me – perhaps curious as to whether I was about to move in on his harem of ewes, congregated on a shady rock ledge nearby.

'Have no fears there, mate...' I muttered.

Amongst the sheep that speckled the opposite hillside, numerous horses roamed. Rather small horses...and zooming in on them with my camcorder revealed rather unkempt brown and grey manes. Surely too unkempt for domestic or working animals. I then realised this was my first sighting of the iconic Dartmoor Ponies.

These animals have resided on Dartmoor for at least three-and-a-half thousand years. In bygone times they were used for not only for riding, but also for shepherding and transporting goods. These days they roam semi-wild and left to their own devices, aside from when they are occasionally rounded up to be sold or moved to other parts of Dartmoor. Being an endangered species, some are used in conservation and breeding programmes. In 1950 there were around 30,000 ponies on the moors. Today only around 1,500 remain, of which only a small number are true pedigrees.

I'd expected to come across these animals sooner or later, but for now I was happy to observe them from a distance. Despite my affinity with the countryside, I've always been a little wary of getting up close and personal with any animal bigger than me. One time as a teenager I stopped in a field on my way home from school to pet a foal. Without warning it reared up at me – but stopped short of planting a hoof into my head. My accompanying friend kindly labelled me with the moniker of 'Horse-Humper' in front of my classmates the following day. In more recent years, and on more than one occasion, I've also been escorted out of fields by angry cows.

Although I've never been overly keen on selfies, as I continued exploring the tor I decided it was high time I got a shot of myself on Dartmoor.

This would be a rare moment of my hike, though. No matter how spectacular my location may be, I always set myself a two-selfie rule on my holidays...and this seemed an appropriate moment for my first. I set up my camera on the tripod and, as the timer beeped away, hurried across the rocks to pose in front of Great Links Tor.

The thought occurred to me after that I should be able to see Brat Tor, my intended final destination of the day, from that location. With its huge stone cross poking out of the top, it would almost certainly be unmissable.

I fished out my compass and scanned over the landscape to the south-west. Almost immediately my eyes were drawn to a small but promising feature. I zoomed in with my camcorder, past the flock of ewes on the rock ledge and down towards the unmistakeable shape of a cross, emerging from the tor some distance away.

Minutes later I said goodbye to Great Links Tor, keeping my eyes peeled for a path to Brat Tor. I also expected to pass by Doetor Brook – or its source, Dick's Well – which was just as well, since I was almost out of water.

Here on the southern side of the tor, numerous narrow paths, worn across the tops of the trenches, made progress much easier than on my approach. I soon came across the infant section of Doetor Brook. And, unlike my previous investigation of a blue line on the map, this led to the discovery of actual *running* water.

I scoured the banks for a gap in the vegetation. Although only a couple of feet wide, the stream had carved an almost cliff-like bank through the rocky earth, forcing me to lay in the cheek-tickling moss to fill my bottle. I doused my sunburnt head, then took another fill, resisting the temptation to take a huge swig. Instead I plopped in a chlorine tablet.

With heavenly particles of Doetor Brook trickling down my face, I headed for Brat Tor and Widgery Cross.

The landmark soon vanished from view as I headed roughly west down the hill. The main route towards the tor, boldly marked by a dotted green line on the map, also evaded me. Instead, the numerous narrow paths that dictated my course would continue only so far before terminating at the end of a steep slope, forcing me to backtrack and change direction.

I continued in this manner for about an hour before reaching a substantial track; presumably another old mining thoroughfare. To the right, the track led back up to Great Links Tor – now shrinking in the distance and losing some of its grandeur, but still dominating the view for miles around. A thin layer of evening mist lingered at its base as the sun crept closer to the horizon. To the left, the track headed south, disappearing amongst the bracken and gorse.

The compass directed me across that track, and minutes later Brat Tor and Widgery Cross popped into view, at the ridge of a gentle hill no more than half a mile away.

Soon I cleared the trenches and found myself back on rocky pasture. The soft glow of the sinking sun caressed my tingling face as it beckoned me to Brat Tor, bathing the landscape in its flavescent light. The sky did its best to compete, only just failing to match it.

The ponies I'd observed earlier now cavorted around me, their long shadows sweeping across the moor, frisking at me in a tease. The silhouettes of other equines observed from a cautious distance, the tips of their tails and manes adorned in a citron glow, before they too trotted down to join the dance.

Golden hour was well and truly upon me. I needed to pitch quickly and start shooting. I could have dug out my camera right there and then, of course, but my instincts told me to get my shelter assembled before the light faded.

As close as possible to the tor, I stooped down and extracted myself from my pack. Unlike the previous evening, camping with discretion would be impossible on this open terrain. But the sighting of a pitched tent down the other side of the hill helped to ease my self-consciousness – whilst another part of me was a little disappointed that I would have to share my campsite.

At first glance, finding a pitch should have proved only a minor challenge. But wherever I found a space free of rocks and excrement, a stab at the ground with one of my puny tent-pegs confirmed the presence of granite only an inch or two below the grass.

Keen to avoid a repeat of last night's battering from the wind, I was determined to have the tent pitched as tightly as possible. My prospects appeared bleak. But after much scouting, and still under the watchful eyes of my welcoming party, I finally found a decent spot and threw up the tent. I hauled my pack inside and extracted my camera.

By my reckoning I had maybe five minutes of this light left before the sun would sink into the belt of mist that clung to the horizon. I contemplated focusing my efforts on the ponies and their shadows, but I also wanted a shot of Widgery Cross and Brat Tor, with the setting sun beside it. This would be the only time I could capture such a sight. The ponies, on the other hand, would no doubt greet me on numerous occasions over these two weeks.

Based on that rationale I made my decision, mounting my camera onto my tripod before hurrying across the rocky plain towards Brat Tor. Once close enough I composed a panoramic image consisting of two shots that I would later stitch together. Then I snapped away. Satisfied with my images, I turned to face the ponies.

Their shadows had lengthened – but were also losing definition as the sun continued to sink behind me. I switched to my zoom lens, seeking out a suitable candidate amongst the frolicking beauties. Just as I found my subject, the last of the golden light disappeared. Along with the shadows.

No longer vitalised in the sunlight, and with the enriching glow stripped from their home as well, the ponies were instantly subdued, like a clockwork toy winding down to the premature conclusion of a performance. They had danced for the fading sun, not for me. Now the dance was over. I turned around just as the last sliver of the sun's orb sank into the mist.

The golden hour had abandoned me too soon. But any photographer who captures every shot he wants is a fortuitous fellow. Over the years I had learned to accept some measure of disappointment during these moments – but on this occasion that absence of fortuity left something of a sour taste in my mouth.

Of course, one could argue that I'd simply made the wrong decision. Perhaps I should have gotten my camera out sooner. Perhaps I'd blown the only chance I'd have during my two weeks to photograph the ponies in such an intimate moment. But only that morning I had told myself there would be moments on this hike that were meant to escape the camera.

Perhaps that evening I had witnessed another one.

Chapter Three: Parasites

Brat Tor to Tavy Cleave

After finishing the last of the couscous I'd pecked at throughout the afternoon, sleep came easily that second night. Aiding my slumber was the fact that despite the exposure to the elements on this rocky plain, barely a breeze drifted across this part of the moor.

Owing to its topography, the sun rises around 15 minutes later on Dartmoor than across most of England. Since I intended to be up in time to witness every sunrise during my hike, that solar anomaly would hopefully prove convenient. I had always been an early riser, too, usually running on about six hours of sleep a night. The 4:45am alarm call I'd set on my phone was therefore no major infringement on my R&R requirements – unnecessary, in fact.

Waking again during the pre-dawn twilight, I cancelled the alarm – permanently – then stretched my weary muscles before extracting myself from my sleeping bag. I unzipped the tent and planted my feet into my muddy boots, which had been banished to the gap between the inner tent and the fly. Without bothering to tie the laces, I grabbed my camera and lurched outside.

A soft, blue tint caressed the landscape, creeping toward the warm hue of the approaching golden hour. A mile or so to the east, the hills were already beginning to transform in colour, like the scaly body of a gigantic chameleon. Shielded by a faint mist, ponies grazed near the bottom of the pasture.

Hoping for a greeting from wispy layers of cirrus clouds, waiting patiently to be painted in shades of amber and crimson, I peered up at the sky. It was filled with lingering stratus; low lying clouds, which during warm weather indicate that rain is on the way. Above this drifted a huge, dark, amorphous mass of grey, moving in at an ominous pace.

I strolled across the dew-soaked grass. To my left, cradled between two gentle undulations of the moor, the sun was struggling to free itself from a belt of mist, in an almost perfect reversal of how I'd watched our star bid goodnight the previous evening. Moments later, whilst oblivious sheep perpetually munched away at the grass, the sun ignited, bringing the sombre sky to life. A familiar, golden glow sprayed across the land, transforming countless drops of dew into tiny torches.

By the time I was done shooting that moment, the yellow tint of the hills was already fading, as was the mist, along with that glorious fireball. Could I squeeze in a shot of the ponies, too? Within moments my answer came, as that swathe of cloud swallowed up the light, leaving behind a dull, listless landscape, devoid of colour and contrast. With a shudder, I headed back to my tent.

As I approached it I suddenly remembered the other tent I'd seen whilst arriving here. I glanced over to where the small dome-tent had been pitched. It was gone. That was some early start by the occupant. An early start I had no intention of emulating. After yesterday's epic stomp I told myself a lie-in was in order – so I snuggled back into my sleeping bag.

At around 8:00am I peeked outside. The cloud had thinned a little but still filled the sky, offering little incentive for me to emerge from my cosy cocoon. Then, whilst assessing my sunburn, I noticed something on my left arm. An insect. A black insect. Big, too. Most of its body poked up from my limb, with two of its three pairs of legs suspended mid-air. A closer inspection revealed the thing's head – burrowed into my reddened skin. It was a tick.

I'd most likely picked it up on Corn Ridge; their prime habitat. Once attached to any passing animal they inject an anaesthetic, allowing them to feast undetected on the blood of their host. Although not usually dangerous, there is a small risk that they may transmit Lyme Disease: a highly unpleasant, debilitating illness which produces flu-like symptoms, sometimes lasting for months.

Generally – as long as they don't try to suck my blood – I'm not squeamish about bugs. In fact, back home I perennially host swarms of ladybirds, taking up residence in and around the wooden windowsills of my flat. Perhaps I'm a more attractive housemate than I give myself credit for. According to social media I probably have a dust-mite infestation. I prefer my own explanation, though...

The tick didn't appear to be alive – until it wiggled a couple of legs at me. The hairs on the back of my neck stood on end and a wave of revulsion ran up my spine.

As I understood it, the thing would fall off of its own accord after a few hours of gorging on my blood. Well, I had no desire to have this critter burrowed into my arm – not for a few hours or a few seconds. I failed to see how the beast would pull itself out voluntarily, anyway, considering how most of its legs and body were hoisted up into the air. I'd also read that attempting to pull them out can result in the head snapping off and remaining embedded in the skin. The recommended solution is to use a special tick remover, which gently forces them out 'without stressing the insect'. Well, sadly for this insect I hadn't invested in one of those. I would be employing good old-fashioned torture.

I snapped on my lighter and held the flame as close as I could to the little bugger. Even though my arm could tolerate the heat only for a few seconds, it refused to budge, simply giving another insolent wiggle of its legs. Next I grabbed the tweezers from my Swiss Army Knife...but still the tick refused to comply. I was convinced the thing would sooner be pulled to bits than surrender its feast, and the prospect of having to extract its severed head from my skin was less than appealing. I admitted defeat – for now – and let the tenacious little sod suck away.

Whilst examining my sunburn, I realised I hadn't seen my own reflection since leaving home two days ago. This prompted me to record a piece-to-camera for my video diary, so I could take stock of my appearance. I fished out my camcorder and filmed myself rambling on about the weather, my progress so far, and my new blood-sucking friend.

I've never been a fan of my geeky, camp voice, but when I reviewed the clip, at the sight of the red face glaring back at me I barely paid any attention to what came out of the speaker. My nose, in particular, was glowing, and my forehead and ears, which I assumed would have been protected by my hat, were not far behind. But despite my sunburn and the presence of my new pet, I was in high spirits, having so far stuck to my planned route, reaching my intended destination on both of those first two days. I had also, therefore, placed my unwavering faith in my map-and-compass skills. An expert navigator I certainly was not, but neither had I ever seen the inside of any search-and-rescue helicopter.

After departing from Brat Tor I would be heading south-east towards the narrow, steep valley of Tavy Cleave, visiting Sharp Tor and Hare Tor along the way. My camping location for my third night was still undetermined. Ideally, I would finish the day near Tavy Cleave, pitching up on the banks of the aptly named River Tavy; one of the most highly rated locations on Dartmoor amongst wild campers. However, I'd also discovered that this location was an area in which, strictly speaking, wild camping was not permitted.

Not permitted??? But I was on Dartmoor – revered as the only place in England and Wales where wild camping is legal...even encouraged! Well, this legislation is not quite as liberal as it sounds. A visit to the Dartmoor National Park website will indeed reveal that wild camping is permitted – but not across the entire park. You will be directed to a map which lists and colour-codes all the areas where wild camping is allowed. Those areas are shaded purple, and at the time of my hike they accounted for roughly half of the land within the national park boundary. Two thirds at best. Furthermore, the military ranges take up a huge portion of that land, and even basic access to those areas – let alone camping – is restricted during the spring and summer months when live firing takes place. Of all the camping locations I'd picked out whilst planning my hike, Tavy Cleave was the only one outside of those purple areas. It was also within the Wilsworthy Firing Range. However, today was Saturday, which meant that whilst camping was *officially* prohibited, there was no access restriction in force. So, upon reaching this area I would gauge how discreetly I could camp. If there was nowhere I could hide myself away, I would have to push on a little further east – which would mean concluding the day with another mammoth, uphill stomp. If possible I would avoid the latter option – but not if doing so might lead to a confrontation with a disgruntled landowner.

The legalities of wild camping in the UK are often debated. In Scotland the rules are clear: pitching a tent almost anywhere is perfectly legal provided you limit your stay to only a few nights and stay well away from any buildings, roads or livestock. Just a few sensitive areas, such as around Loch Lomond, are exempt from this rule, where byelaws have been introduced to try to curb excessive camping. In England and Wales the rules are just a little ambiguous. Officially, on any land south of the Scottish border, permission must be sought and agreed by the landowner before you pitch your tent. However, in certain areas – the Lake District, for example – wild camping is tolerated. Veteran campers will tell you that in these areas, provided you follow the wild camping code of conduct, you face little risk of being moved on. In any case, except in cases where damage has been caused, prosecutions against wild campers are rare.

I was not a veteran wild camper – so I would be taking no chances. If camping discreetly at Tavy Cleave appeared problematic, I would just have to move on. Simple as that.

With planning over, my thoughts turned to breakfast. My appetite had undergone something of a renaissance since the previous afternoon. However, breakfast today would be a less lavish affair than that of 24 hours ago. Scarcely enough water remained in my bottle to prepare both tea and porridge, let alone wash up – and there was no stream anywhere in the vicinity of my tent. An insignificant blue line wriggled across the map about half a kilometre north of Brat Tor. Slightly further away was Doetor Brook. For the sole purpose of cleaning my saucepan, though, I lacked the inclination to seek out either of them. Neither did I fancy having to scrape congealed scraps of porridge from my saucepan later on. So I decided I would forgo my oats, compensating with extra custard creams to dunk in my tea. Fortunately, I am always prepared to compromise my affluent lifestyle...

After breakfast I strolled up to Brat Tor. From the base of the rocks I surveyed the outskirts of the national park to the west, where the moor dropped a little steeper before blending almost seamlessly into a patchwork of meadows and farmland a few miles away. In every other direction the moorland rolled on and on. As for the tor, this stack of granite bore the same bluey-grey colour as Great Links Tor, but took on a more abstract formation, with cracks appearing to split the rock in a crude, grid-like pattern. Consequently, and probably for the best, I was unable to recycle the food analogy I'd conjured up the previous day in regard to its neighbouring tor.

Widgery Cross, poking out from the top of the rocks, served as the runaway attraction here. So much so that I couldn't resist taking another selfie, although I told myself it would definitely be my last. Besides my aversion to them, I needed to be mindful of my battery power until reaching the campsite in four days' time. But I could spare enough juice for one more, so I set my camera on the tripod, framed my shot, then negotiated a route up the rocks

With its granite-block construction (ten of them in total), as opposed to having been carved from a single piece of stone, Widgery Cross is unique amongst all the Dartmoor crosses. It is also the largest, standing almost thirteen feet tall and spanning four-and-a-half feet across. The cross was named after William Widgery, born in the Devonshire village of North Molton, in 1826. After training as a stonemason he went on to become a prolific local artist, painting over 3,000 pictures of Dartmoor. In the latter part of his life he lived in the village of Lydford, just a mile or so from where I stood, where he built a house and art studio in 1880. That property is now the Lydford House Hotel, offering some of Dartmoor's most highly-rated holiday accommodation. Widgery died in 1893 – just six years after commissioning this cross in honour of Queen Victoria's Golden Jubilee.

Clambering up beside the thing involved something of a precarious climb, but once up close, with my tee-shirt flapping wildly in the wind, I could fully appreciate the skill and tenacity required to construct such a landmark. I struck a triumphant pose and sucked in my gut, then pressed the button on the camera's remote control – only to discover I was out of range.

Back down I went, to move the camera closer and try again. Then, with the second – and definitely last – selfie of my hike done and dusted, I headed back to the tent to pack up.

By the time I was ready to leave Brat Tor it was nearly 11:30am. Quite a late start – but I was confident I could reach Tavy Cleave in no more than four hours. For one thing, it was only about four miles away.

Four miles in four hours. Sounds shamefully easy, doesn't it? But after yesterday's stomp, which totalled...wait for it...about FOUR MILES...I figured I deserved an easier day. Also, in my defence, I was carrying a *lot* of weight, and fast learning that around these parts the difficulty of the terrain crossed was the fairest factor upon which to judge one's progress – not the distance. I was already pushing myself hard enough. That mile-and-a-half or so between Corn Ridge and Great Links Tor was the toughest stint of walking I had ever undertaken in my life. My objectives over these two weeks were simple; enjoy what Dartmoor could offer and expand my photography portfolio. That was it. And let's not forget, the latter of those two objectives also necessitated frequent stops, inevitably restricting my daily mileage.

To reach Tavy Cleave I would head south, before climbing east up Rattlebrook Hill to Sharp Tor, passing Doe Tor along the way. From Sharp Tor I would cross a ridge to Hare Tor, then head down to Tavy Cleave. There were no paths marked on the map to cover this route, but from what I could see of the hills ahead I would be crossing relatively smooth pasture most of the way.

The moorland soon turned rough again after I set off, forcing me along assorted faint paths that had probably seen infinitely more hooves than human feet. I then reached a more substantial stretch of Doetor Brook, which I wouldn't have attempted leaping across even without my pack. After filling my bottle, I followed the brook downstream, crossing it at a stone footbridge. I then adopted a more defined path across Doetor Common, crossing the Walla Brook via another stone bridge. This easy terrain compensated, almost, for the incline, and by mid-afternoon I reached Doe Tor.

Nowhere near as impressive as its larger cousins, Doe Tor proved to be the first such landmark to leave me feeling a little underwhelmed. What was of interest, though, was a battered old sign attached to a nearby flagpole, warning me that I was about to enter the Wilsworthy Military Firing Range.

The British Army has been using Dartmoor as a training ground since around 1800 – originally to hone their musket skills, in order to guard the 5,000 or so French and American prisoners of war incarcerated within Dartmoor Prison. From the 1870s onwards, troops were a regular presence near Okehampton. In the 1890s the Okehampton Artillery Practise Camp was constructed, which included stables large enough to house over 700 horses. Some of these buildings still survive today, now accommodating soldiers rather than equines. In the early twentieth-century, further land was given over for the training of troops in the use of small artillery. Following the outbreak of the Second World War, the army commandeered almost all of Dartmoor. In the year before the D-Day landings, US troops also trained here. By 1945 the War Office had requisitioned nearly 80,000 acres of the moor, with over half of those permanently closed to the public. Military appropriation of Dartmoor gradually reduced, and in 1951, Dartmoor National Park was born. The popularity of the moor grew, and throughout the 1960s so did concerns over the risks posed by derelict buildings, craters, military debris and unexploded ordnance. In 1973 the army's holdings were reduced again to around 32,500 acres. That number remains unchanged to this day – and live firing now takes place on only 22,000 of those.

Only 22,000 acres. That's still a little over 34 square miles in which some weary rambler might wind up being accidentally shot if they happened to miss the warning signs, and ventured past the line of red-and-white posts that crossed the hill not far in front of me. Assuming, of course, that the sound of gunfire had failed to divert them.

The sign stated that if a red flag was flying from the pole by day, or a red light illuminated by night, then I was not to cross the posts. Having checked the access dates whilst planning my hike, I knew there would be no flag flying today. The sign also warned against touching any military debris – or 'it may explode and kill you'. I wondered if anyone had ever been injured or killed on these ranges. Ironically, this part of the sign bore what appeared to be a bullet-hole.

I later learned of numerous military-related tragedies upon Dartmoor. One of the most documented cases occurred in 1901, when the mutilated bodies of three men were discovered a few miles away near Yes Tor. They had been blown to pieces by a bomb. Such was the force of the blast that one of the men's feet were found 200 yards from his body. Nowadays it is standard practise to have the ranges cleared of any dangerous materials after every firing exercise. Consequently, there have been no further tragedies for many years.

I turned around to gauge my progress. The massive Great Links Tor was still visible in the distance. Brat Tor was closer but distinctly smaller. Then I noticed the silhouette of a human form standing alongside Widgery Cross. This was my first sighting of anyone in nearly 24 hours. I zoomed in on the figure with my camcorder. The highly magnified image shook wildly on the screen, but clearly distinguishable was a man with a walking pole in his hand. Judging by the tiny rucksack on his back, he clearly hadn't set out on any hike on the scale of what I was attempting. Inadvertently, a slight smugness swelled within me.

That smugness soon fizzled away as I set off on the last and most laborious section of the climb up Rattlebrook Hill, crossing the line of posts into the firing range. As usual, my body demanded frequent rest stops, but I eventually stepped up onto a rocky ledge and the hill climbed no more. Sharp Tor now loomed over me.

Sharp Tor was perhaps a little larger than Brat Tor. Structurally, though, the cracks in this stack of granite again rendered my cookies-and-pancakes analogy obsolete. But even assuming my appetite had still been alive and kicking, the appalling stench of this location would have certainly killed it off. Because dumped over the whole area was the greatest concentration of bovine excrement I'd ever seen. The beasts that had deposited it had since vacated the area in search of fresh pasture down the other side of the hill.

The ridge between Sharp Tor and Hare Tor dipped as I proceeded towards the latter. This next tor took on a more rounded form, although I was unable to agree with those who had described these rocks as taking the form of a crouching hare. Nevertheless, the views on offer from Hare Tor were impressive in every direction.

From here I traced the entire route I'd taken since about 7:00pm yesterday. As the crow flies, roughly a mile-and-a-half away to the north stood the ever-present Great Links Tor. Sharp Tor perched relatively close before me, flanked by the dark specks of cows. Thinning clouds projected crawling shadows across the moorland. In the centre of my field of view, either Arms Tor or Little Links Tor preceded Brat Tor, with Widgery Cross now barely visible. Further still, a visage of the moor's western edge seeped through the haze, whilst on the opposite side of this vista the moors rolled onward to the east. Behind, to the south, the squashed valley of Tavy Cleave lay about a kilometre away, still shielding the river, whilst Ger Tor rose high above to the right. Beyond, a stretch of the river snaked through more hills, greener than those in any other direction, from which sprouted patches of deciduous woodland.

After resting up at Hare Tor I began to head downhill towards Tavy Cleave – and if all went to plan there would be no more walking uphill that day.

The nearer stretch of the River Tavy crept into view. Branching from it, alongside a small weir, was a mine leat – a narrow, man-made stream. I was slightly taken aback by the presence of a few walkers enjoying a stroll along a well-trodden path, the route of which apparently included a footbridge that crossed the weir to a long, narrow island. Whether or not I would be able to camp down there now looked even more uncertain.

Minutes later the gradient levelled off notably as I passed a rocky outcrop, where Rattlebrook Hill met the edge of Tavy Cleave. A short, gentle descent to the riverbank presented on my left, whilst a couple of hundred metres straight ahead, the moor climbed up to Ger Tor, keeping watch over the valley below.

Suddenly the sunlight burst through the clouds, washing over the landscape. The river transformed into a blinding slash of white. This illumination multiplied my desire to get down there – so much so that I instantly lost any inclination to check out Ger Tor, despite the marvellous views it no doubt offered across the Tavy Valley. Instead, applying little consideration as to the best way to reach the riverbank, I headed straight down the hill.

As the gradient eased, the grass darkened and my boots began to squelch. Up ahead, a wide marshy area blocked the path for a direct descent. Had I checked the map ten minutes earlier I would have noticed the blue line that indicated a stream…or another strip of sludge, courtesy of some dribble of a well nearby. Inexplicably, and just like the 'stream' on Corn Ridge, the fact that water seeped from the earth and piddled down to the river via the mud warranted a name and a blue line on a map.

But this was no time to be splitting heirs; it was still an obstacle. An obstacle I should have identified sooner. Of course, I could have simply gone back up the hill and detoured around it – but something told me to stick to my guns and find a route across. My adventurous streak, perhaps. Or my new-found dislike of walking *up* hills. Or just plain stupidity. But so close to the river, and bolstered by my triumph over that marshy mess yesterday, I struggled to find a reason why I might fail here.

I began to weave my way across, seeking out the least-soggy patches. But the Green Hedgehogs were proving to be less obliging, here. Pulling my feet from the mush became more gruelling with each step as I drew closer to the river.

Then the midges returned.

At this sudden distraction, I paid less than perfect attention to the selection of my next step – and down I went.

Wet vegetation crunched beneath my torso. The stiff leaves of a hedgehog-plant clawed at my face. An expletive escaped my lips – although I managed to keep the volume restrained, instead investing all my energy into a pathetic swipe at the midges. My cheeks flushed as a wave of embarrassment gushed through me, but that feeling dissipated as I began to formulate a plan to get up.

As had often been the case, I would have to manoeuvre onto all fours. I pulled my feet from the sludge, anchoring them against a tussock, then heaved my pack around so I could lay on my belly. I positioned my hands and knees over the firmest vegetation, then pushed. My hands sank into the cold, green-brown mush. The hedgehogs squirmed beneath the combined weight of myself and my pack. That cool, wet sensation replicated at my knees as I shifted my feet around to secure a better grip. I pushed harder still…and moments later the world's worst explorer was back on his feet.

I scanned the area as the midges continued to harass me. Fortunately those ramblers I'd seen earlier were long gone, so at least there had been no-one around to witness this debacle. Mud covered much of my right leg from the thigh down. The other had been largely spared.

Due care and attention was resumed, and eventually I reached firm ground on the other side of the hedgehogs. A wry smile crept across my face as I glanced back over my route – then at the strip of dry, smooth grass that led straight down to this spot from the edge of Ger Tor. I brushed bits of grass and leaves from my clothes, then proceeded down to the riverside.

Below Ger Tor, the shallow river stretched to about 20 feet wide. The mine leat joined it beneath a small concrete building alongside the weir. Many leats had been constructed on Dartmoor during the industrial revolution. Many of them remain in place, though they are now largely redundant. This one was fast flowing and just a few feet wide, maintained by a thick, waist-high stone wall on its left bank, running alongside the path. On the other side of the leat, the valley climbed steeply up to Ger Tor, covered in impenetrable bracken.

I crossed the bridge over the weir, proceeding to survey the island I'd observed from the hillside. This would have made a beautiful camp; flat, smooth and with plenty of space for alfresco dining – should I wish to have porridge oats blown all over me again. Best of all, of course, would be the view from my tent, with the river trickling past me on both sides and the narrow gorge of Tavy Cleave up ahead. But the glaring issue was the footpath just a stone's throw to my left. Reluctantly, I rejected this spot and crossed back over the weir, heading downstream.

The path stuck close to the leat on my right, allowing a strip of wild heathland to separate the path from the riverbank on my left. As the path gently descended, the leat maintained a level altitude along the hillside, creating the subtle illusion that the stream was somehow flowing uphill.

The remains of a drystone wall crept up to the left of the path, partially closing off the heathland. The state of the wall could perhaps be attributed primarily to walkers' boots. Now I was about to make my own contribution to its ever-so-gradual demise. But somewhere down there, my pitch awaited me. The thought occurred to me again how, strictly speaking, I wasn't really supposed to camp here. I also felt a little guilty for following in the footsteps of those who had crossed the wall before me. On the other hand, considering its dilapidated state, the wall clearly no longer served any purpose. Neither was there any signage anywhere stating that the strip of heathland it bordered was private property. This fact alone made a poor defence, though, so I consulted the map. I already knew camping was prohibited – but there was no indication that any part of the riverbank around here was excluded from public-access land. The whole area still fell well within the thick yellow line that bordered such areas, so as far as I was concerned, I was permitted to explore it at my leisure.

Scanning the heathland, I spotted a little clearing that might do for a pitch – although being only about 20 metres from the path, it would offer little by way of cover from the beady eyes of passers-by. But there was no way I was going any further today.

Just as I was about to make my way down there, another group of walkers began to approach from the opposite direction. Fearing I might arouse their suspicions, I dawdled along the path, pretending to be fascinated with the hillside flora. They pretended not to notice my filthy trousers as they passed, leading me to contemplate making a light-hearted quip about how this was my version of midge-repellent (I'd seen Bear Grylls plaster himself in mud to demonstrate this on TV), but I kept it to myself. The thought did bring a smile to my face, though, which the walkers mirrored half-heartedly as I stepped aside on the narrow path.

I dithered until they were out of sight, then brushed the dried mud from my legs. In this weather, and as thin as they were, my trousers would dry super-quick, and the residual stains would be inconspicuous. The only aspect of my appearance that I was becoming self-conscious about was my sunburnt skin…but there was nothing I could do about that.

I clambered down onto the heath through one of the gaps in the wall, finally disposing of any sense that I was trespassing, then weaved my way through the thick grass and bracken to my potential pitch. Following the briefest of inspections, and despite the sloping ground, it met with my approval.

Within moments of getting my pack off, the midges set upon me again. I threw up the tent in record time, although as usual the earth proved too rocky for most of the pegs to penetrate deeply. Neither was there room amongst the bushes to fix any of the guy-lines in place. I shoved my pack inside and practically dived in after it, then yanked the zips home, sealing myself off from the parasitic mob outside.

I stretched out inside my sanctuary, shuffling around until the lumpy ground no longer protruded into my back. I lay motionless for ages. I ached all over. For the first two-and-a-half days of this hike my body had been running mostly on adrenaline; all I'd eaten in about 36 hours was a tiny tub of couscous, some tea and biscuits, and half a bar of chocolate. But oddly, I still had almost no appetite.

I also stank, reeking of a combination of body odour and mouldy vegetation, with notes of sheep shit thrown in for good measure. I'd brought along a few basic toiletries and had brushed my teeth every morning, but otherwise I hadn't washed since leaving home. Neither had I changed my clothes. I told myself that a wash in the river tomorrow morning, along with some fresh attire, would be the perfect way to get the serotonin flowing through my brain again.

I stripped naked. My socks, filthy and damp down to the heel, were the last items to come off, releasing a feeble crackle and a puff of dust as I peeled them from my feet. I did have one observation to be grateful for; although cracked and flaking like a sausage roll, my toes remained free of blisters.

I lay back down on the cool groundsheet. Whilst soothing to my bare back, it emphasised the prickly heat of my sunburnt head and arms.

Then, remembering that tick, I glanced down at my arm. The

thing was still there, poking its ass up at me defiantly. I had neither the energy nor the inclination to do anything about it.

Could I keep this up for another eleven days? Physical exhaustion, I could forgive myself for. But I had also been making errors of judgement; silly mistakes that I would never have made on any of my previous hikes. But this terrain – and this level of exertion – were new territory to me.

I told myself yet again that I had not come here to kill myself. If I was going to struggle to reach my overnight spot, or those camping legalities were to prove problematic, I would simply camp elsewhere. Only one fundamental rule governed my hike: it was imperative that I reached my booked accommodations at the end of my first and second weeks. All other plans were subject to change.

Exhaustion and paranoia would *not* get the better of me.

As if on cue, there then came a shuffling noise from outside the tent.

Frozen with fear, I expected a thump on the flysheet at any moment, followed by a stern voice ordering me to pull up my polyester monstrosity and vacate the area immediately. Perhaps accompanied by the sound of a shotgun being pumped. As my heart raced, the noise shifted from one side of the tent to the other. But that voice never came, and after a minute or two the noise went away. I told myself off again; it was most likely nothing more than an inquisitive sheep.

I sat up to reach for my camcorder, wincing as my bare back peeled away from the groundsheet. Then, for the second time that day, I examined the assortment of pixels that recreated my face on the screen. Although the sun had barely made an appearance until the late afternoon, my head seemed even redder than it had that morning.

After dispelling my demons with a lazy rebuke of myself, I settled in for the night. It was only a quarter-past-eight, but there was no way I was going back outside to be feasted upon by the midges.

This meant I wouldn't be having a proper dinner, either, as

cooking inside the tent would be neither safe nor practical on this incline. I wasn't fussed about cooking, anyway. I settled for the remainder of the chocolate bar I'd started earlier.

I scrunched up my clean clothes into my usual makeshift pillow, then lay down my tingling head.

I didn't even consider going out to take any photos as sunset approached. Neither could my book offer me any consolation, and I was still too paranoid over my location to dare to turn on the radio. As dusk drew in, I lay still in the fading light, and told myself that tomorrow would be a better day.

Chapter Four: Sustenance

Tavy Cleave to Harford Bridge Campsite

Due to the incline on which I'd pitched, I awoke the following morning to find myself slumped halfway down the tent with my feet pressed against the polyester. I shunted myself back up the mat and lay dozing; last night's hiatus from photography would carry over into this morning, too.

But today was going to be bath-day. I contemplated surrendering my wash in exchange for a lie-in. But this could be the only decent opportunity to clean myself up a bit before reaching the halfway point of my hike.

Reluctantly I wriggled out of my sleeping bag, then dug out my toiletry bag, towel, and a clean pair of boxer shorts.

Then, alerted to the expectation of another midge attack as soon as I unzipped the tent, I suddenly remembered the other parasite that had been feasting on me – for well over a day, now.

I peered down at my arm. The little git was still there.

Not for much longer. I dropped my pants and toiletries and reached for the tweezers again. 'I am not a walking blood-bank,' I muttered.

I seized the bug by its bloated body and gave a slow but firm tug. As before, the tick refused to comply as my skin stretched from my arm – leading me to further doubt that it would come out in one piece. Perhaps it would pop, splattering a gooey mess all over my arm in a final act of vengeance. Its tiny legs wriggled in protest as I pulled a little harder, twisting the tweezers slightly to give the beast an added incentive. Then out it came – and in one piece.

Its legs wiggled as the thing presumably pondered its fate. The head was too small to reveal any features – such as the mouth that had imperiously sucked at my flesh for the past 36 hours or so. I could afford a *little* sympathy, though. It was only trying to survive, after all. I felt slightly flattered, even. Clearly I had served as a delicious meal – one that was far too tasty to surrender without a fight. But I wasn't getting overly attached; I unzipped the tent and un-ceremoniously tossed my guest out into the bushes.

Although I'd pitched only a few metres from the river, the thick undergrowth prevented me from getting close to the water, so I would have to use the exposed stretch near the weir to freshen up. Surely, with the hour approaching 7:00am, the riverside would be deserted…

I stepped out beneath an even mix of blue sky and fluffy fair-weather cloud, although the narrow valley hadn't yet escaped the shade of the hills. The heath alongside the river was alive with birdsong. Neither were the midges as bothersome, now. Perhaps today *would* be a better day…

Then, out of nowhere, a man appeared, strolling along the path – heading towards my intended bathroom. Although he was too distant to see me crossing the heath behind him, his presence was enough to convince me that stripping naked in the river could lead to an awkward encounter. Frustratingly, I conceded that I would have to compromise.

I scampered up onto the path, filled my bottle in the leat, then scampered back down. I stood poised behind a bush, peeping through the foliage. Once the man was out of sight I gave a last look in the other direction. The coast was clear. I quickly stripped off, then half-emptied the bottle over my smelliest, dirtiest extremities.

I gasped as the cold water spilled over my flesh, then wedged the bottle between a couple of rocks and fished out my peppermint shower gel from my toiletry bag. I massaged the stuff into my armpits, then headed south...

This style of washing wasn't *totally* alien to me; back home my bathroom wasn't equipped with a shower, so my morning routine usually began with me standing in the bath pouring jugs of water over myself. Owing to my insanely expensive, electric immersion-heater, a bath – with bubbles and everything – was restricted to a weekly treat.

I worked my way down to my feet, where the gentle scratching of grit accompanied the sting of soap penetrating the cracked skin between my toes. I rinsed myself off and, after a quick rubdown with the towel, slipped into a fresh pair of boxers, before dragging my shorts and boots back on.

My flabby, naked belly jiggled about freely as I hopped back to the tent. My pale torso contrasted sharply with my tee-shirt-suntan arms; burnt bright red up to the elbows, then resembling the skin of a frozen chicken thereafter. What a magnificent celebration of the human form I was.

Back under cover of polyester, I put on some fresh clothes. With regards to my attire I reckoned I'd packed reasonably light for nearly a month of living in a tent. My supplies consisted of two pairs of ultra-thin hiking trousers (featuring zip-off lower-legs, should I at some point fancy showing off some more flesh); three tee-shirts; a long-sleeved check shirt; a black fleece-top; three pairs of boxer shorts; three pairs of thick socks, and my waterproof trousers and jacket.

My wash, although only rudimentary, had invigorated me. I packed up quickly – but I wasn't leaving Tavy Cleave just yet. Whilst I had foolishly overlooked its potential at dawn, leaving this beautiful little valley without a few shots in the bag would be unthinkable. So, with my full gear in tow, I headed back up to the weir for an alfresco breakfast, to be followed by a photography shoot.

After devouring the last of my custard creams and a saucepan of porridge, I picked out a shooting position in the shallows of the river, close to the weir and the island I'd surveyed the evening before. The right of my composition featured Standon Hill – a steep climb forming the eastern side of the valley. On the left, before the start of Tavy Cleave-proper forged its way through the earth, the gentle section of Rattlebrook Hill, where I'd misjudged my route down here, climbed up to Hare Tor. Right-of-centre and further upstream, the river curled and disappeared into the cleave, above which a slice of distant moorland sat wedged between the steep sides of the valley.

Whilst adjusting my tripod, and as the shallow water trickled over my boots, my peripheral vision detected a baseball-capped figure approaching briskly along the path. After a subtle glance or two I became convinced it was the same man who had cost me my luxurious bath earlier – presumably walking a circular route, as he was heading in the same direction as before. Although maybe 20 years my senior, his muscles bulged through a pair of grey shorts, a matching tee-shirt, and an unzipped, thin blue jacket.

He drew level with me on the bank and came to a halt. Suspecting he may have witnessed my earlier bathing session, or spotted my tent and realised that I'd camped here, I pretended not to notice him and continued with my tripod adjustments. The latter of those two suspicions swelled within me as he stood there, perhaps watching me...perhaps not. In seconds my suspicion engulfed me. Blood rushed to my cheeks. Considering the default colour of my face, though, my reaction had most likely gone unnoticed.

'Morning!' he said, cheerfully. 'Beautiful day for it, eh?' He nodded at my camera. 'I got a coupla nice ones meself earlier, of the sun comin' up over the top 'o' the hill.' He pointed towards the hill he'd referenced, which sat snugly within the frame of my shot. 'You 'ad much joy?' A touch of a Devon accent laced his exuberant tone.

'Well, I was a bit too lazy to be up that early,' I quipped, engaged by the discovery of our mutual passion, whilst also slightly jealous of his photographic success – although he didn't appear to be carrying any camera gear. I could only assume he'd used his phone. I was annoyed with myself for abandoning another dawn photography session – that was two out of three mornings lost. Or was I expecting too much of myself regarding my photographic ambitions? Yes – my photos were massively important to me. But that didn't mean I should be depriving myself of sleep on a daily basis, especially after such extreme exertion. I was also still committed to the philosophy that not every beautiful scene should be captured on camera – although a part of me still lamented over that missed chance to photograph the ponies near Brat Tor.

'This is my first shot of the day. I'll see what happens,' I added, amiably.

The man nodded towards my open pack nearby. 'Did you camp 'ere, then?'

My brain froze. Just as my cheeks had begun to cool, blood gushed into them once more. There was little point in trying to deny it. Besides, this chap's friendly nature had stripped me of any wiles I may have once possessed.

'Yeah...just for the night,' I confessed, bracing myself for the onslaught.

'Can't beat it, can ya...? I'm ex-military so I know these moors like the back of me 'and.' With unwavering enthusiasm, he remained oblivious to the odd blend of anxiety and kinship our conversation had imparted on me. 'Anyway, good luck!' He nodded and smiled again, then headed off.

'Cheers...' I replied, a little bewildered.

I gave a limp wave, but he'd turned his back to me already, heading for the cleave and leaving me slightly bemused that he hadn't minded one bit that I'd camped here.

Having not actually explored the cleave yet, I considered following him. But that might've made me look like a bit of a weirdo. Besides, heading that way would take me away from my intended route, and most of the morning was already over.

I turned my attention back to my camera, and as soon as my friend had vacated my composition and disappeared into the depths of Tavy Cleave, I captured my shot.

Much of that day's route would present quite a change from what I'd gotten used to over those first three days; after following the river a little further downstream I would be temporarily leaving the moor, heading south-east for a few miles along a couple of country lanes, before rejoining the moor at a place called Cudliptown Down. Whether I would camp there or a few miles further at Great Staple Tor had yet to be decided. My other option was to follow the river upstream through Tavy Cleave, then take on a steep ascent to the top of Standon Hill, then across another area labelled on the map as 'bracken, heath or rough grassland'. Memories of Corn Ridge had flashed through my mind as I'd scanned that little portion of the map.

At that moment I realised that I quite liked paths.

I packed away my camera gear and headed downstream.

I crossed another line of red and white posts. A flagpole bearing the warning sign about the firing ranges followed, only this time confirming my exit from the Willsworthy Range.

As the temperature climbed beneath the midday sun, I paused near a cattle grid to empty my water bottle over my head, before taking my final opportunity to refill it from the leat. By this point the river had deserted the path, and now the leat, too, was about to curl away to the north.

I soon arrived at a deserted, gravelly car park at the end of a lane. Then, for the first time in days, my feet met tarmac. The soft thud of my boots on the road was more welcoming than I'd anticipated, as was the presence of trees and hedgerows, offering some precious shade.

Passing rows of pretty houses, I began to mull over the fact that four days into my hike, I was yet to have a poo. What was happening to my digestive system? I could only assume that because, breakfasts aside, I was functioning on rather meagre rations, my body was squeezing every last joule of energy from anything I swallowed; nothing was going to waste. I just hoped this quirk of my metabolism wouldn't desert me anywhere within the vicinity of these posh country houses.

I followed the undulating roads for a little under two miles, passing through the hamlets of Higher Wilsworthy and Hilltown, before reaching a bridge crossing the River Tavy, now wider and flowing with a little more gusto as it approached another weir. Here I temporarily abandoned the road, pausing at a small nature reserve; a strip of deciduous woodland flanking one side of the river.

The heavenly aroma of barbecued sausages and burgers wafted by as I sat on a fallen tree trunk; a young family were enjoying a picnic a little further upstream. Fortunately, the super-sized bowl of cement I'd wolfed down that morning was still satisfying my stomach, otherwise I may have been tempted to raid their cosy little picnic. My thoughts of sausage-pillaging I could repress only for so long, however, so I pushed on over the bridge.

Bypassing the western edge of the moorland, the country lanes had led me mostly on a gentle descent – which could mean only one thing after crossing the bridge: the road began to climb. Gently at first. Then less so. The shadows of the hedgerows no longer fell in my favour, either, affording me little respite from the heat. Rather pathetically, I stopped for another rest – no more than ten minutes after my last break. But, keen to improve my rate of progress, after hopping down from a gate I willed myself to the top of the lane without stopping. Mercifully, my route then turned left at a tee-junction and I was back on a more or less flat gradient. Soon my detour was over; I turned off the road onto a bridleway. Then, beneath a huge oak tree, I paused to rest. Again.

Whilst refreshing to feel a road beneath my feet for a couple of hours, my temporary absence from the moor had disconnected me from my wild experience. I'd felt exposed; denounced. But as I passed a stable, where a glossy black horse studied me from behind a gate, uneven stones and ratifying dirt greeted my feet. Right about then the sky began to cloud over, too, offering some respite from the sun.

Mark Newman – a.k.a. (almost) the world's worst explorer, was back in the game.

Soon the trees and hedgerows either side of me disappeared as the bridleway opened out onto Cudliptown Down. Countless hooves had weaved a faint scar across this stretch of the moor, heading south-west and bypassing the boulder field of White Tor, which, although yet to make an appearance, lay about a kilometre away. To the left of the bridleway, smaller rocks peppered the earth all the way up the hill. A few remote houses dotted the landscape in the distance. Behind them, to the south, the moorland faded into the near-constant haze on the horizon.

I considered heading straight up to White Tor. However, six tors had already crossed my path so far on this hike (or seven if you include Branscombe's Loaf – a tor by structure if not by name), and the appeal of 'Tor-Hopping' was beginning to wane. So, after refilling my bottle in the tiniest of streams, I continued along the bridleway.

White Tor crept into view on my left. It bore the usual blue-grey hue of other tors but wasn't particularly striking – lacking in the gravity-defying or haphazard features of its predecessors. Like I had seen at one or two other tors, a tall mast poked above the rock. This one seemed more prominent, however, somewhat spoiling the untouched-by-man impression the other tors had evoked.

The lightest sprinkling of rain began to tease my bare forearms. I removed my hat, and then felt a light stippling upon my scorched scalp.

To my disappointment, the shower passed within minutes, and after steadily climbing for half an hour or so, the hillside levelled off almost flat, where I paused to take in the impressive 360-degree views. Still I remained rather indifferent to White Tor – although it was predominantly around those rocks that large numbers of ponies and sheep had congregated.

The moor descended gently to my right, merging into a tapestry of farmland in the distance, amongst which lay the pretty village of Mary Tavy. Beyond stood Brent Tor, with its famous Church of St Michael at the top – one of the highest-altitude churches in England. Most intriguing, however, was the view to the north. Recognisable by its distinctly rounded form was Ger Tor, guarding the descent into Tavy Cleave, along with part of the wider Tavy Valley that I'd passed through via those country lanes. Even more impressive were the three un-mistakable, rocky bulges of Great Links Tor, still refusing to bow to the horizon almost two full days since providing the backdrop to my first selfie.

Despite the plentiful hours of daylight that remained, the seductive views led me to question if I should camp here rather than carry on towards Great Staple Tor. I had some way to go to reach it. Neither did I have any idea how difficult the approach would be – other than the fact that it would inevitably include another big uphill stomp.

And I was getting hungry.

This was the end of the road for today.

Camping right on the bridleway would be unappreciated by any passing riders, though. The grass either side of the route wasn't particularly thick, but dome-shaped bumps covered most of the ground; an indication of some old cultivation practise, perhaps. Nevertheless, I managed to find a patch just about even enough. And for once, the earth was soft enough to hammer the tent pegs all the way into the ground.

Soon the clouds cleared again and watery sunlight bathed my camp. Faint shadows drifted across the distant fields, diluted by the haze as the green and yellow tones of the countryside melted into one another. As I surveyed this vista, with my saucepan of rice gently simmering away, I struggled to justify my anxiety of the night before, over what had really been only minor concerns. But despite the discovery of my newest nirvana, I lacked the enthusiasm to get out my camera, preferring to simply observe and absorb all that enveloped Cudliptown Down.

Sometime later, the intermittent sound of galloping hooves, distant at first and then much closer, broke the silence as I lay absorbed in my book inside the tent. A peek outside revealed three ponies, including a foal. Presumably they'd ventured down from White Tor, curious about their guest.

The sky had turned a subtle shade of pink; the hills near Brent Tor a fading, misty undulation. The trio of beauties snorted and scampered around, encircling my camp much like they had done on my arrival at Brat Tor, only this evening the sunlight struggled to penetrate the haze. Even so, a soft, familiar glow adorned the ponies' white and grey coats, whilst long blonde manes, unkempt yet elegant, dressed their heads, reminiscent of the mullets of one or two eighties pop stars.

As the ponies began to make another approach around my right flank, I grabbed my camcorder and started filming what would surely make a lovely clip for my video diary.

The youngster led the charge, taking great delight in butting into the others, leading me to wonder how all those legs didn't tangle together, bringing them all crashing to the ground. Then they came to a halt, glancing back and forth in my direction. Moments later their eyes fixed on the red bulge poking out from the strange, green shape that had encroached onto their territory.

I zoomed in slowly, keeping my hands as steady as possible to minimise camera-shake. My eyes flitted between the ponies and their onscreen presence, whilst the graceful animals stood silently swishing their tails, alternating the subject of their stares between myself and someplace beyond.

What lay behind those enigmatic brown eyes at that moment? Did they regard me with suspicion, curiosity, indifference? Judging by the considerable attention I was now receiving, that third option seemed the least likely.

Whilst still staring straight at me, one of the older ponies lifted his tail and a pile of shit fell from his ass. Then the three of them trotted back up to White Tor. I snapped the camcorder screen shut with a giggle, contemplating how I might edit that video clip.

The wind awakened me on the fifth day of my Dartmoor adventure. Wind that alternately whistled through the rocks of White Tor then thumped between the layers of my tent. In the dawn twilight I took a peek outside. Thick, charcoal and ink-blue clouds filled the sky.

I zipped up and lay back down.

Later on came more trotting sounds. Were the ponies returning for another toilet visit? But these hooves produced rather a more rhythmic beat; a far cry from the random thudding that had drawn my attention the previous evening. I peeked outside again.

A woman was approaching on horseback.

I shouldn't have been surprised; I was camped right alongside the bridleway, after all. I tried to look casual as the rider drew nearer, dressed in a pair of black jodhpurs and boots, topped by a dark blue jacket. Since she must have seen me by now, the option of retreating into the tent seemed ignorant. Before I knew it, the horse's powerful legs, glossy black coat and beautifully brushed mane were passing right by me.

'Morning,' the rider greeted, smiling. Curly brown hair poked out from beneath her helmet. I hadn't put my hat on, so my ridiculously-orange bonce was on full display.

I responded in kind, sensing – to my relief – that she wasn't intending to stop for conversation.

Out of nowhere, a Labrador, wearing the same glossy black coat as his equine companion, came rollicking up to the tent, sniffing and panting. Suspecting I was about to be slobbered upon, I jerked back inside. The dog showed virtually no interest in me, however. My other fear involving the cocking of legs also proved unfounded.

'Trix, come on...sorry!' the rider called out, glancing back without stopping. I put up my hand to give her (or him...is 'Trix' a female name???) a stroke – but at the sound of her (or his) owner's voice, Trix romped away.

I watched them trot down the other side of the hill until they were out of sight, perhaps heading for those stables I'd passed the day before.

I then spread out the map to review the day's itinerary. Today I would continue south to Whitchurch Common. The main attraction here was another stone cross – Windy Post Cross, to be exact. Not as large and imposing as Widgery Cross, by all accounts, but judging by the photos I'd seen, this landmark and the surrounding moorland certainly warranted a visit.

The B3357 traversed the entire width of the national park – one of only two main roads to do so. Conveniently, any logical route to Whitchurch Common from here would incorporate a stretch of that road. Convenient because a mile or two along it, the Dartmoor Inn served hot food and traditional ales – and after four days of dining on my meagre rations I planned on treating myself to a pub lunch.

Oddly, though, something still suppressed my hunger. Had my brain just become too hotwired to think about *real* food? Or had the monotony of my diet over the past few days simply killed my appetite? Well, regardless of my hunger levels, I just wanted to feel some decent grub slide down my gullet – so why shouldn't I indulge in an hour or two of gluttony? Just a couple of hours, out of the 336 of them, give or take a few, during which I would call these moorlands home…

After breakfast I nipped out to fetch water. The nearest stream trickled across the bridleway about half a kilometre down the hill. My trousers and shirt flapped submissively in the wind as I strolled along, following the fresh line of hoof-prints that had been laid less than an hour ago. My tracking skills didn't extend to paw prints as well, though.

However brief, I always relished any chance to take an unencumbered stroll without my pack. A red sore was beginning to wear onto the skin where the straps had been rubbing my shoulders. My back, however, had become largely accustomed to the load after that first day, and had since only begun to ache in the late afternoon, recovering by the next morning. My feet, despite their tenderness and the cracked skin between my toes, had yet to show any sign of blisters. My main physical concern had been my knees – but even they'd held up so far. So, in short, I was doing all right. On the other hand, this was largely down to the fact that I was purposely keeping my daily distances short. But that was easily justifiable; after hiking all the way to Ivybridge, I needed to have something left in the tank for my trek along the coast.

Sensible. That was the appropriate word to summarise my approach to this hike so far. Well, sensible-ish, anyway.

Reaching the stream, it became apparent that the muddy, feeble dribble here would be inadequate to fill my bottle. I left the line of hoof prints and headed upstream, quickly abandoning that trickle and moving onto another stream. Then another. Then another… Eventually finding a current that necessitated a wide step to cross it, I scraped out a gap in the gravelly bed and squeezed my bottle beneath a tiny waterfall. Then I turned around to head back to the bridleway.

It was nowhere to be seen.

Neither were the other streams I'd surveyed. I headed downstream, scanning the hillside for anything that would give away my route up the hill, but in the absence of any bushes, trees or rocks, retracing my steps even over this tiny area was impossible. White Tor, a little over half a kilometre away, was the only identifiable feature reasonably close by. About the same distance away was the opening of the narrower stretch of the bridleway, where it joined Cudliptown Down before disappearing beyond the hedgerows. But it would have been ludicrous to walk all the way down there just to get back onto the bridleway.

I wandered around and picked out another few miniscule streams, following each in turn. Eventually, and after spending a far greater amount of time searching for the bridleway than I had searching for a water source, my third option led me back to the muddy puddle that crossed the lines of hoof prints.

Cudliptown Down was nowhere near remote enough a location upon which I could become *really* lost, though. If need be I would have simply headed up the hill to White Tor, where I would have surely spotted the bridleway – maybe even my tent. Nevertheless, that moment of carelessness jostled with my grey matter as I strolled back up the hill. Especially as I planned to be crossing much more remote areas of Dartmoor in a week's time.

After packing up everything else, I stood and watched my little tent battle with the wind. So far, erecting and un-erecting it had presented me with no real problems. Was I overdue a challenge in this respect? My pondering came to an abrupt end when my rolled-up camping mat took off, blown away down the hill. I gave chase, almost resorting to a rugby tackle to pin it down, then secured it beneath my pack.

I returned to my convulsing tent and began to dismantle it. The thing flapped with increasing ferocity as I wrenched each peg from the ground. After removing the last, I tugged the flysheet from off the inner tent. It leapt high into the air, tangled guy-lines in tow, like the resurrected corpse of a huge, dismembered kite. I let it flap wildly for a few moments before hauling it to the ground. Despite my best efforts, the undead kite refused to return to the grave. Eventually, though, I managed to reduce its size to the width of the bag, before laying on top of it and writhing around like a petulant child, forcing out the trapped air. I stowed it under my pack and turned my attention to the newly-naked inner tent, which now thrashed about like a bunch of chimps caught in a net. Deconstructing this followed a similar narrative as the flysheet, with the rear end resembling a pair of giant water wings as I battled to force the air from that, as well. Eventually I managed to get the whole thing rolled up and zipped inside the bag.

'Come on!' I said, jubilantly flipping the bagged tent onto my shoulder as I got to my feet.

The clouds fizzled away as I headed down the other side of Cudliptown Down, transforming the drab morning into the makings of another beautiful day. At the bottom of the hill I came across an ancient, weathered marker stone, engraved into the base of which was the letter 'S'. The map named this feature as Stephen's Grave – which I later discovered was the subject of a Dartmoor legend... Around 300 years ago, a local man named George Stephens, driven to despair by unrequited love, poisoned the object of his affections. Consumed by guilt, he then took his own life. As was common in those times, it was forbidden for suicides to be buried on hallowed ground, leading to his burial here instead of in a churchyard. There are a few variations on this story, but all of them conclude with a warning that his ghost can often be seen patrolling this area after dark.

Yet more evidence, perhaps, that I was better off remaining a singleton.

I left George Stephens in peace and continued for a mile or two, departing Cudliptown Down before passing a trio of hills capped by Roos Tor, Cox Tor and the aforementioned Great Staple Tor. Then I reached the B3357. Here I turned left towards the village of Merrivale – and a little closer to my scrumptious lunch.

The road climbed briefly then levelled off, revealing glimpses of Whitchurch Common through the trees and shrubs lining the tarmac. Approaching a significant viewpoint, the flora cleared, allowing a panoramic vista across the common to the hills. Before them, amidst clumps of trees, the stumpy rocks of Vixen Tor poked up from a shallow valley. To my right, a stream passed beneath the road through a culvert, disappearing amidst the moorland after carving out a smooth gulley. Innumerable ponies and sheep completed the scene, with a team of the former species concentrated around a rocky outcrop below the ridge of a hill.

After taking a few shots I sat beneath a blossom-draped hawthorn tree near the culvert, watching the animals graze whilst fluffy clouds drifted overhead. Further along the road, vehicles frequently slowed to dodge cattle and ponies which, unrestrained by fences, and blissfully ignorant of the traffic, had wandered onto the tarmac.

With the risk of missing out on a lunch service growing ever more present in my mind, I forced myself to get moving again. Though if need be I would still settle for a pint and a bag of pork scratchings. I might even scoff down the hairy ones, too…

Approaching Merrivale, the road dived into a small, wooded valley, in which the tiny village sat. Then I spotted the pub: a large white house, set behind a small car park and an open-plan garden. Although furnished with a few benches, a couple of strutting geese were the lawn's only occupants. The words 'Dartmoor Inn' had been painted on the front and side of the building, in a black, Olde-English-style font.

Wondering if I might pick up a signal, I switched on my phone. It now displayed four signal bars, so I phoned my mum to let her know I was still alive. I told her about the weather; the terrain; how much sleep I'd had; what I'd been eating (I lied on this subject, reassuring her that I'd had three cooked meals every day). She laughed when I told her about my dormant bowels. Once she was no longer fearful of my fate, I concluded our chat and headed for that yummy lunch.

The geese, penned into a chicken-wire enclosure, paid me little attention as I crossed the pub's garden. A welcome sign hung above the door. Another hung from a post, bearing a painting of a tor – though I didn't recognise it as any of those I'd visited. Finding the door locked, I peered through a window. The clean, white décor was inviting, as were the immaculately-laid dining tables. But the place was deserted. I peered up at the first-floor windows. All the curtains were drawn.

The Dartmoor Inn was closed, with no indication of its opening times. Rather cruelly, a sandwich board stood in the garden, taunting me with its promise of 'delicious home-cooked food'. Having been a city-dweller all my life, I'd failed to consider that most rural pubs don't stay open all day long.

I wolfed down my last chocolate bar, then headed back up the road towards Whitchurch Common, soon abandoning the B3357 in favour of a path that would lead me to Windy Post Cross.

The monotonous whoosh of road traffic gradually faded away, leaving behind only the sounds of birdsong and the whistling wind, as the rolling moor forced the air upwards and through the tors – which, no matter where you were on Dartmoor, never seemed to be far away.

Further along the path I was surprised to discover swathes of charred gorse bushes – no longer decorated with their tell-tale yellow flowers, but instead shrivelled and blackened, like giant, barbecued bugs. I'd read that on parts of Dartmoor the spread of vegetation is managed with controlled burns, but this was the first time I'd come across any sign of such activity. Whilst in principal I've always been opposed to humans interfering with nature, the moorland has been managed this way for hundreds of years, with these burns playing a vital role in keeping the landscape from becoming overgrown and inaccessible – a fact that toppled me from my moral high horse as I proceeded across the common.

After negotiating a huge puddle, I came across a team of a dozen ponies or so grazing right on the path – seemingly oblivious to my presence as they sought out edible morsels amongst the scorched bushes. Most of the mature animals resembled those I'd seen the previous evening, with uniform coats of white and grey, and scruffy manes. The youngsters, however, were a little more resplendent, with large light-brown patches across their creamy coats.

At just half a dozen or so metres away, this was the closest I'd gotten so far to any Dartmoor ponies. The bracken and gorse weren't thick enough to prevent me from bypassing the animals, but I was curious as to how they might react if I passed between them. As it turned out they were most accommodating, trotting out of the way once I stepped a little closer. Some gave me a sideways glance – but that proved to be the extent of their interest.

Shortly after passing them I reached the cross.

Windy Post Cross (or Beckamoor Cross, as it is also known) failed to impress in the way Widgery Cross had. Leaning to one side, it stood just over two metres tall, and had been carved from a single piece of granite. Its exact origins are unclear, though most historians date it back to the sixteenth century. It is believed the cross served as a waymarker for an east-to-west route across Dartmoor, linking the abbeys of Buckfast & Tavistock. It had been assigned the name of Windy Post on account of its battering from the harsh gusts of the common. Its elevation of 300 metres above sea level gave credence to this name – although I can't say I felt anything more than a light breeze as I stood before the landmark.

As the stream alongside the cross gurgled away, I gazed back over the gorse-peppered common. In the distance, Cox Tor and Great Staple Tor capped the hills I'd passed that morning en route to the road (of which there was no sign at all anymore). Next to the cross, a footpath forded the stream above a tiny waterfall, before heading for the rocky outcrop of Feather Tor, a few hundred metres away. In the mid-distance, Vixen Tor revealed just a fraction more of itself than my earlier glimpse. The moor climbed modestly on my left, to where the silhouettes of ponies dotted a ridge about a kilometre away.

After taking a break I began searching for somewhere to pitch. Caution was required, though; as best as I remembered, I was either right on the border of an area where camping was allowed – or just outside it (I'd brought along a copy of the map that detailed such areas on the national park website…but after spilling my morning cuppa over it on the third day, it was mostly illegible). In the half-hour that I'd sat by the stream I'd observed numerous dog-walkers, joggers and cyclists…but how many of them would know where the exact border of that purple area was…?

First I scouted the other side of the stream, finding a great little secluded spot where the ground sank into a clearing, probably twice as deep as the height of my tent and encircled by bushes. No-one would ever know I was there unless they stood just a few metres away. Pitching so close to the water, though, would be serving myself up as a delectable feast for the midges. Reluctantly, I ruled that spot out and crossed back over the stream.

Whilst eagerly inspecting other potential pitches, a faint odour of something burning wafted through the air. I then saw smoke rising to the south, perhaps a kilometre away. The source was unclear. Was there another controlled burn going on? In the absence of any warning signs, that seemed unlikely. As did the possibility of my being caught in a raging inferno in the middle of the night…

Nestled amongst a few bushes, a couple of hundred metres or so from the cross, I eventually found my pitch. Not as discreet a spot as I'd hoped for – but it would suffice. My theory about escaping the midges by camping away from the stream also fell to the wayside; they came out in force as soon as I removed my pack.

Once the tent was up, I took refuge with my book for a while before preparing dinner: another bland saucepan of rice. At least the variety of flavours I'd brought went some way to minimise the banality of these meals. Tonight it was beef. Perhaps if I took the stodge for a stroll, the burning moorland would add some smoky, barbecue flavouring to it? Like when those *Masterchef* contestants lift up their cloche-covers to reveal a rump of beef sweating amidst a cloud of hay smoke...

Or maybe not.

In truth, though, the rice, whilst far from being my ideal choice of meal, was palatable enough. Those sachets had served as my main foodstuff during most of my camping trips – though normally I would spread those meals out with the odd can of soup or baked beans from a campsite shop. The couscous, on the other hand, had become hard to swallow – quite literally. I'd passed on the stuff after eating it cold on that second day, opting to snack on biscuits and chocolate instead. Now I was out of chocolate, and my biscuits needed to be rationed for breakfasts only. On a positive note, tomorrow afternoon I would be arriving at a campsite and relaxing in a little bit of relative luxury. And stuffing my face with some *real* food.

After dinner I wondered what photographic opportunities the setting sun might offer me – although after five days and four nights, I was beginning to understand the nature of the Dartmoor climate. As sunset approached, I stepped outside. Another evening haze had descended, depriving the land of shadows, muting its colours and rendering the sky featureless. Images of the moorland set beneath vacuous skies, I already had aplenty.

Once again my camera remained in its bag that evening.

The night was calm and the air still. Feeling relatively alert in comparison to previous mornings, I awoke shortly before dawn. After performing my stretch routine I lumbered outside with my camera gear – where I was finally introduced to the fog this landscape is famed for.

In my experience, fog usually resulted in either absolute triumph or dismal failure when it came to photography – rarely was there any grade of success between. This fog was different from any I had ever seen, sweeping across the moor in bursts of thick, luminous clouds. To the east, an intense glow radiated above the hills, smearing the division between fog-bound earth and sky. Already losing its golden tint to a dazzling white, the glow indicated the sun had breached the horizon somewhere within, unable yet to escape its cocoon.

After observing the clouds repeatedly smother then release Feather Tor, in a semi-hypnotic state I hurried down to the cross. The fog surged at me in swathes, each time reducing visibility to just a few metres. As I reached the stream, the glow to the east condensed, pinpointing its solar source with greater accuracy.

The valley that housed Vixen Tor became the last refuge for the fog as it refused to accept the inevitable. The clouds were lifting, losing pace and definition. Occasionally they parted – sufficiently slowly for my eyes to behold, yet too quickly for my camera to capture adequately in the low light. My tripod would permit a longer exposure, of course, but shooting at such a setting would sacrifice the definition of the clouds.

Like dying fingers, the last few wisps of fog caressed the hills near Merrivale. Finally they accepted their fate and slipped away. The thin cloud protecting the fog followed, exposing the still, textured layer of its cirrus counterparts high above, allowing the wan sunlight to seep through and tease the partially-charred gorse bushes.

That moment heralded my final shot of the dawn.

I analysed my shots over breakfast. A handful stood out as keepers. A couple had great potential. Then, out of the corner of my eye, I noticed the tent pole wobble slightly. Then came the sound of a snuffling animal. I unzipped the flap. Hooves thudded. I poked my head outside. A couple of equine legs disappeared behind the bushes.

The beast had had its lips around one of the guy lines – evidenced by what I could only assume was pony saliva: a white goo, glinting on one of the lines in the pale sunlight. Whilst I'd been half-hoping for some intimate engagement with the ponies, this wasn't exactly what I'd had in mind. Had I not zipped up the tent when I'd ventured out earlier, I might have returned to find one of them burying its nose into my bag of oats. Had it opted for the couscous, I probably wouldn't have minded.

I made that morning's breakfast the most leisurely yet, and the discovery that my coconut ring biscuits had been battered to pieces during transit put only the slightest dampener on proceedings. I also discovered a few small blisters starting to form on my feet. This was of no major concern, either; a well-stocked first-aid kit was one of the few items in my pack that I'd given careful consideration to – including a selection of special plasters and pads to protect my tootsies.

As usual I was in no rush to get moving – but today, for once, a lazy start was justified; as per general campsite etiquette, the one I was heading to wouldn't allow me to pitch before lunchtime. I would also be backtracking across Whitchurch Common along the way, so it wasn't as if a late departure would lead to my missing out on any new sights.

I would be staying at Harford Bridge Campsite, still within the boundary of the national park but just off the moor, a few miles north-west of Whitchurch Common. A few other, closer sites were marked on the map, but during my research I'd discovered they were all either no longer operating, or catered for caravans only, or were ridiculously expensive for one lonesome backpacker with a tiny tent.

I set off back towards the road at about 11:00am, this time taking a path roughly following the stream. I paused near the culvert to take in the common one last time, then proceeded along the tarmac, soon turning onto a quiet lane.

As I trudged along it dawned on me that I would soon be engaging in my first significant human interaction in days. Hopefully my armpits and ass-crack weren't *too* rotten. Whitchurch Common couldn't offer the same level of discretion as the bushes near Tavy Cleave, so I'd abandoned the idea of having another wash that morning. I wouldn't be the first sweaty, smelly, red-faced hiker the locals had encountered around these parts, surely...

After stomping on, mostly uphill, for a couple of miles, I reached Harford Bridge and crossed the River Tavy for the third time in four days. Halfway across I paused to glance down at a few static caravans, not far from the riverbank at the edge of the campsite. A thick layer of trees lined both banks of the river, parting on one side for a small pebble beach, where a couple of young boys were ankle-deep in the water, dragging toy fishing nets through the swift current. They peered up at me curiously for a moment, then returned their attention to their nets as I stomped over the bridge.

I passed some pretty little holiday cottages, then minutes later I reached a driveway, where a bold sign declared my arrival at the Harford Bridge Campsite.

Chapter Five: Relative Luxury & Momentous Moments

Harford Bridge Campsite...and Wheal Betsy

The driveway was sandwiched between a wooden cabin marked RECEPTION on the left, and a large square lawn, neatly bordered by shrubs and pretty flowers, on the right. My boots clumped across the veranda of the cabin as I approached the door, where a bell tinkled to announce my entrance.

The reception doubled as a shop and carried a faint scent of pinewood. A woman stood behind the counter. Officious-looking. Middle-aged. A tanned face and black, shoulder-length hair. She wore a black polo shirt, boasting some logo on the breast pocket. A pair of horns, or maybe horseshoes, framed around the number 30...? The number of years they'd been in business, perhaps...?

She was midway through serving a customer, ringing up his purchases on the till whilst haggling with a supplier over the phone. Her authoritative tone, along with the staccato beeping of the till, chopped through the faint hum of a chest freezer parked under a window behind me.

A plethora of canned foods crammed the shelves lining the walls. Soups; hot dogs; baked beans; stewed beef; chilli con carne; spaghetti hoops; peach slices in syrup – or in juice if I fancied going upmarket. What really caught my eye, though, was the fridge standing at the back of the store, stacked with cold drinks, dairy products, and fresh meats. Alongside it stood a freezer, piled high with assorted lollies and ice creams.

A wire rack stuffed with postcards stood next to the door. I couldn't resist comparing the images on display to my photographic efforts. I'd like to say mine stacked up – but of course, they didn't. The printed images had been captured with pro-equipment, and crucially, by better photographers. They mostly featured various tors set against beautifully coloured clouds at sunset. The only locations I recognised in any of them were Brat Tor and Great Links Tor. Although a little downhearted by the superior quality of the competition, I reminded myself that I was barely halfway through my hike; there was no telling what photographic treats lay ahead.

The woman behind the counter concluded the phone call and her transaction with the customer almost simultaneously.

'Hi there!' she enthused, in a slightly shrill tone as the customer left. 'Sorry to keep you, are you looking for a pitch?' I stepped forward – but only slightly – wary of how my unsavoury odour would easily bury that sniff of pinewood.

'Yeah, there should be a reservation, two nights. The name's "Newman."'

'Okay...let's...have...a look...' She dragged the words out almost teasingly as she opened a large folder, running a finger down a list of names. 'Ah, yes. Here you are. Mr Newman. And I see you've already paid in full.'

'Actually, would I be able to extend that to three nights?' I hadn't given any thought to extending my stay as I'd sauntered along the driveway. This snap decision could perhaps be attributed to the allure of the potential feast on offer behind me. Or to the sweat that oozed from every pore of my aching body.

She flicked between pages of the register. 'Err...yes...' Her enthusiasm faltered for a second. 'That's no problem at all.' She glanced at my pack. 'You haven't driven here, have you?' She posed this question as if it were a matter of national security, prompting a chuckle from me as I replied in the negative. Her spirited timbre bounced back: 'As you're hiking you qualify for our discounted rate for backpackers, which covers the extra night.'

She seemed to underplay this monetary fact – perhaps hoping I wouldn't catch on to her subtle admission that had I not requested to extend my stay, I would have paid more than I'd needed to. I recalled no option to select any 'backpacker discount' when I'd paid a whopping £36.20 in advance for only two nights.

I certainly wouldn't describe myself as tight-fisted. I'll always reach for my wallet when it's my round – but at the same time I've always been thrifty with my finances. This skill I've honed particularly well over the past few years, having frequently spent months at a time unemployed between bouts of agency work, after being made redundant from my lacklustre career in the insurance industry. My modest lifestyle meant I could stretch out my meagre life savings considerably during this period; the rent on my studio flat was peanuts; I didn't drive; I was single; I had no debts; I had no family to support, and I had a limited (but just about sufficient) social life.

Where I really excelled at saving the pennies, though, was in my food budget. On many evenings I would head round to the nearby supermarket to raid the reduced-to-clear shelves of the chilled and bakery sections, once everything had been marked down to ten or twenty pence. This would sometimes require a degree of dogged determination amongst the throng of other desperados, who suffocated the poor store assistant as he set to work with his pricing gun, but usually I would come away with one or two prizes. Certainly that evenings dinner. Sometimes the following day's lunch, too. On occasion I would emerge victorious from the crowd with a whole basketful of goodies.

The Christmas and New Year period was often a bonanza; on Boxing Day it was a foregone conclusion that there would be a stack of crates waiting for me, filled with Brussels sprouts and parsnips, whacked down to silly prices. Free, even. The same would apply in regard to mince pies. One year I bought 24 boxes of them in two days. On the second day I bumped into my mum and step-dad in the aisles, who were somewhat bewildered at the contents of my shopping basket. 'I like mince pies' was the only explanation I offered.

From that stockpile I devised the groundbreaking 'Mince pie and Milkshake Diet'. As the name suggests, this consisted of eating nothing but mince pies and a well-known brand of dietary milkshake. This followed the 'Noodle and Milkshake Diet', which I'd also invented a year or so earlier, incorporating a well-known brand of an instant noodle snack (this 'diet' actually proved surprisingly successful. The mince pie version, less-so).

Even though contributing little to the shrinkage of my waistline, the mince pie diet offered other benefits; since it cut down on my cooking needs I saved electricity, helping to reduce my carbon footprint. As well as my obscene energy bills. Everyone's a winner…

I'll admit that shopping for food in this way tugged at my pride just a smidgeon – but it was always worth it if it helped keep me out of those languid temping jobs a little longer. I certainly didn't live hand-to-mouth, either; my spending habits were a matter of choice. And I still allowed myself a weekly treat, when I would go crazy and cook myself something from scratch. Toad-in-the-hole; lamb madras curry; chilli-con-carne; spicy parsnip soup; roasted red-pepper houmous. These were just a few of my specialities.

I was content with my lifestyle over this period, and each time I clocked out on my final shift at another inconsequential job, any sense of uncertainty I may have felt was tempered by the sense of liberty and excitement at whatever plans I'd concocted for my latest sabbatical.

During this period I enjoyed more financial freedom and lack of responsibility than I had throughout most of my adult life. Now I just needed to figure out how to balance my lifestyle with some sense of fulfilment – a task that had become ever more urgent as I approached middle age. Before sitting down to plan my Dartmoor adventure, I came to realise I had sedately slipped through the last ten years or so of my life. Out of nowhere, my forties were bearing down on me. I needed some excitement. My passion for photography wasn't quite enough – so this trek across Dartmoor would mark the beginning of my long, midlife crisis avoidance programme. A programme I am still very much enrolled in.

After exchanging a few final pleasantries with the receptionist, I headed down to the field to find my pitch, clutching the rudimentary map she'd handed me. Dotted about the place were a dozen or so camper vans and caravans. There was no sign of life around any of them. The few pitches neighbouring mine, which collectively encircled a verge of long grass surrounding a tree, were all vacant. My tent would be the only one in the field.

Once pitched, I nipped over to a tap near a hedgerow to fill my bottle – something of a novel task, considering the water supplies to which I had become accustomed. Whilst the tap burbled away I peeked into the neighbouring field. It, too, was sparsely populated. But of course June was outside of the peak season. A week or two into the school summer holiday, this place would no doubt be heaving.

I strolled over to a clearing in the trees at the edge of the field. A vague path weaved down to the riverside. Nettles and cow parsley concealed the water, however; its presence confirmed only by the sound of a trickling current.

An ideal spot, perhaps, for skinny-dipping.

I would explore the riverbank properly some other time – though I very much doubted this would involve taking my clothes off. For now, I just wanted to stretch out in the shade. On some flat, smooth, excrement-free grass.

This stopover at the campsite wouldn't be a complete rest, though. Tomorrow I would be visiting Wheal Betsy – an old abandoned mine building up past the nearby village of Mary Tavy. This walk would constitute a round trip of about six miles. No great distance – but one that would actually prove the highest daily mileage of my hike so far. It would also be the least-strenuous day so far, as all I would be carrying anywhere for the next two days would be my camera gear.

My stomach began to growl as the afternoon wore on, so I strolled up to the shop, returning with a big bottle of zesty refreshment, an ice cream, two packs of bacon rashers, half a dozen bread rolls, a bottle of ketchup, and a disposable barbecue. I scoffed down the ice cream before it could melt, then lit the barbecue.

Once the flames had reduced to a pile of white-hot powdery coals and a few red embers, I ripped open the packs of bacon and laid out as many rashers as would fit onto the grill. Almost immediately they began to sizzle and spit as plumes of smoke wafted into the air, entwined with their juicy aroma. I wondered if the heat would last long enough to cook the lot, but last it did, and soon I'd amassed a mouth-watering pile of crispy-edged rashers, spread out on the hessian-like carrier bag I'd been given at the shop. My saliva glands began to spasm as I sliced open a roll with my Swiss Army Knife, before loading it with four rashers and drizzling them with ketchup.

I devoured that first roll in minutes. Two more followed, finishing all twelve rashers.

I was stuffed. They were, by some distance, the best bacon sandwiches of my life. I took a hefty glug of my fizzy drink, and after expelling a massive burp I didn't move for ages. If that lot wouldn't finally kick my dormant bowels back into action, nothing would.

Later, as the evening drew in, and once my bloated belly had recovered from my gluttony, I headed back up the drive to check out the facilities and brush my teeth.

The inside of the shower-and-toilet block was clinically clean and air-conditioned. Once done marvelling at the décor, I took stock of my appearance in a mirror over the wash basins.

My reddest feature was still my nose, now peeling at the tip. The rest of my face was also glowing, except for a pale border around my eyes, courtesy of the light-reactive lenses of my glasses. My lips were dry and cracked, and skin was peeling from my cheeks, too – although a week's worth of stubble disguised this to some extent. The disguise was also starting to spoil the definition of my goatee beard, though. I'd packed a disposable razor so I would fix this at some point during my stay.

My neck was giving my nose a run for its money, as was my scalp – despite the fact that I'd been wearing a hat most of the time. That bump on the head at Okehampton Castle had left a hard scab in its place, but since the morning after sustaining it, I'd felt virtually nothing of that injury. I pulled the neckline of my tee-shirt aside to study the red band branded onto each shoulder by my pack.

The face staring back at me was of little surprise. That nose, though, was too conspicuous for my liking. So, at the cost of a slight sting, I peeled off the crusty flakes of skin and rinsed them down the sink. I wasn't here to enter any Dartmoor beauty pageant – but neither was I prepared to parade myself through the village tomorrow displaying some kind of ridiculous reptilian hooter.

Back at the tent, I lifted up the cooled, ash-filled barbecue to reveal a rectangle of blackened grass beneath. Eager to get my feast underway, I'd forgotten to raise the tray off the ground. Earlier on I'd walked past a stack of bricks near the bins, in front of which a sign labelled them specifically for this purpose.

David Attenborough once informed me that grass is one of the toughest organisms on the planet, capable of recovering from even the most devastating wildfires that sweep across the African savannah every year. So, whilst regretful of my cock-up, I was quite sure the grass would recover from my devastating barbecue.

And as I'd seen first-hand, a bit of fire didn't seem to do the moor any harm.

I dozed lazily the following morning, until visions of an intense stream of water and a cloud of steam began to shimmy through my fuzzy brain.

Not long after, I stepped into a shower cubicle and stripped six days' worth of filth from my skin. A slight sting, courtesy of the soapy water dousing my heat-sensitised scalp and the cracked skin between my toes, was all that dampened this cathartic moment.

Fully cleansed, I headed back to the tent for breakfast. Despite that magnificent feast the previous afternoon, any urge to visit the toilet was *still* unforthcoming – and remained so after my usual serving of porridge. Still confident, however, that this would be the day of my rectal awakening, I decided to wait before heading out.

I washed my saucepan and spork.

I checked the weather forecast.

I dressed my blisters and brushed my teeth.

I bagged up my dirty laundry.

I tidied the tent and threw away my rubbish.

Still no awakening. So, armed with a toilet roll squeezed into my camera bag, I set off to find Wheal Betsy.

Down by the Harford Bridge I joined a section of the West Devon Way – the same trail along which I'd bid farewell to Okehampton on my first day. After passing alongside a pretty cottage I crossed a stile. The path then opened out onto a small meadow, before leading me up a hill.

From the hilltop, the Tavy Valley offered lovely views to the east, overlooking lush, sheep-speckled pasture on the other side of the river, divided by thick hedgerows and sprayed with patches of woodland. In the foreground, a winding ribbon of trees concealed the route of the river along the valley floor. Although a stark contrast to what I'd become accustomed to over the past week, this view held its own against the wild moorland.

In the next field, the views incorporated the village of Peter Tavy, perhaps a kilometre away and dominated by the conspicuous grey tower of its church. I stopped for a moment to take a photo. However, this appeared to be against the wishes of a herd of cows grazing nearby; as soon as I started snapping they began sauntering towards me, some with their heads lowered menacingly. At first I paid them little attention as I fiddled with my camera. Within moments they were metres away, eyeing me intently.

I'd witnessed how temperamental cows could be – especially in early summer after the calving season. Once I'd even seen a herd of them chase two dogs around a field after their owner had ignored a sign warning him to keep pets on a lead. Eventually he managed to rescue and leash them. Then, in a bid to escape a tense standoff, he was reduced to roaring like a lion at the aggrieved cattle, jumping up and down and bulging out his arms like a freshly-transformed Hulk. From the safety of a neighbouring field, I watched in amusement until his performance just about had the desired effect, allowing him and his pets to make a swift exit.

My dalliances with cattle had been far less dramatic – so I showed little concern as these beasts guarded their field, glaring at me unwaveringly. That was until one of them – I guessed a juvenile judging by his size – performed a bizarre hopping stunt from the front legs to the back, accompanied by a loud snort.

Taking that as my cue to leave, I rushed for the stile that crossed a hedgerow into the next field. To an overture of snorting, I scampered up the steps, expecting to feel slobbering mouths nipping at my legs. I was spared, however, and at the top I turned around to see the field's disgruntled residents gawking at me with varying degrees of malevolence.

I bid farewell to the bad-tempered bovines and continued along the West Devon Way, crossing through more lovely (cow-free) meadows for about half an hour. The path then dropped into a little wooded area, crossing a brook before leading me out onto a lane.

After passing through the outskirts of Mary Tavy village, the lane joined the A386 that crosses the western fringe of Dartmoor National Park from north to south, linking the towns of Tavistock and Okehampton. Wheal Betsy was a little over a mile away up this road. But bubbling up from the recesses of my brain were fantasies of that delectable pub lunch that had so far eluded me. According to my map, not one but two pubs, about a kilometre apart, lay waiting for me along this road…

Arriving at the first of them – The Royal Standard – I was greeted by boarded-up windows and a jungle of weeds protruding through the car park.

I headed further down the road.

After passing a coach-hire business, a post office and a general store, I reached the Mary Tavy Inn. My glimpse through the window revealed fully laid tables. But the door was locked. Then I saw the sign confirming their opening times.

Thwarted again, I settled for a hot pastie (far more preferable to couscous) from the village shop, then resumed my walk up to Wheat Betsy.

As the A386 began to climb, I veered off onto a track, passing a private little wooded area. I then turned a corner and promptly came to a halt. A flimsy wire fence was all that separated me from two huge highland cattle – with long, curved horns protruding from their heads.

They glared right at me.

I was beginning to sense this wasn't to be my lucky day for animal encounters.

Such feeble wire would never hold back these leviathans – then I noticed a sign attached to the fence, depicting an electrocuted hand.

I opened the gate to an almighty creaking, then stepped into the lair of the beasts. They came a few steps closer. The painful racket repeated itself as the gate slammed shut under its spring mechanism. Giving the hairy monsters a wide berth, I headed swiftly across their paddock – this time with no sounds behind me to indicate a pursuit. Exiting the field, I glanced back at its residents. They gazed back at me blankly.

Wheal Betsy was certainly an intriguing structure, standing twice as high as a suburban house – due in part to the massive, round chimney that climbed up one wall and reached a good few metres above the tip of the gables, leaning slightly to one side. As one might expect, the whole building appeared to be constructed of granite. A few square holes, seemingly placed at random, breached the sides. Former windows, presumably. A nearby placard detailed the history of tin mining in the area. This was an engine house, operational, on and off, from 1740 until 1877, until advances in mining technology meant the site was no longer economically viable.

After pondering over how that wonky chimney had withstood the savage Dartmoor winds for over 260 years, I turned round to take in the view across the valley.

Trees smothered the hillsides and most of the stream at the bottom, which would have once been utilised to extract tin ore from the earth. I traced the route of the track I'd detoured from on my way here, which weaved downward, crossed a bridge, then climbed back up the other side of the valley, before opening out onto the grounds of a riding school, where horses grazed in a field. At the very top of the valley the trees gave way to smoother pasture, and beyond that rolled the familiar moorland that dominated the horizon throughout this part of Devon.

After taking a few shots I took the path back to the road. My hairy, horned friends had moved to another part of their enclosure and paid me little attention on my second passing.

Reaching the village, I popped into the shop again for more

supplies – chiefly, four cans of cider – then headed back to the campsite.

I spent the rest of that afternoon sprawled out beneath the shade of the tree by my tent, whiling away the hours with my book. Despite the absence of the isolation the moors had provided, the almost-deserted campsite still offered some privacy – even though I'd returned to find that a young couple with a baby had pitched up on the other side of my tree. But if I lay down outside the tent, the verge of long grass around the tree made for a decent partition between us.

I struggled to concentrate on my book, though, frequently abandoning it in favour of watching the insects in the grass. The exploits of an earwig were particularly amusing. It had captured a beetle of some kind, and was now presumably carrying it back to its nest to gobble it up. The prey almost dwarfed the predator…but still the earwig stumbled on, with its meal securely tethered to its back by the pincers protruding from the rear-end of its body.

Later on, after I'd finally engaged with my book – specifically, John Lydon's account of the tempestuous relationship between himself and his Sex Pistols bandmates – the sky suddenly darkened. A few heavy splats of rain hit my chest. I put down my book and observed a massive grey bulge creeping overhead. My fellow campers were taking shelter, except for an elderly couple who remained seated within the awning attached to their van. As the rain intensified, the young couple rushed out to grab their shiny, multi-ringed stove from off a picnic bench.

I simply sat cross-legged, invigorated by each drop of water that plopped onto my face and arms. But blue sky was already returning on the eastern horizon. While I still could, I flicked off my hat and watched the raindrops patter onto my tee-shirt.

Like the growls of a pack of wolves encircling their quarry, a rumble of thunder ricocheted across the sky. I tilted my head back, eagerly anticipating the next rumble as raindrops stippled my face. That next rumble never came. Having barely dirtied their claws, the wolves had retreated. A few minutes later so did the rain, and the campers who'd taken refuge re-emerged from their vehicles.

Soon after came another distraction from my book: the sound of soft footsteps approaching. I glanced up to see the old man who'd been sitting in his awning all afternoon, now strolling towards me, dressed in an all-beige combination of sandals, shorts, short-sleeved shirt and a canvas hat. His wrinkled but tanned face was hard to read, but suggested he had surpassed his seventieth birthday.

He stooped down in front of me.

'Just so you know, if the weather gets rough there's plenty of room for you to kip in our awning if you like.'

His tone was amiable, delivering an accent that suggested he was a fellow west-midlander.

'Oh, right...thanks!' I replied, enthusiastically, trying to hide my surprise at his offer. 'That's good of you. I'll be alright though. It's not proper camping without the rain.' I threw in an appreciative grin.

He nodded, as if he knew something I didn't, before gesturing towards his vehicle. 'Just in case it gets a bit shitty, all right...'

'Cheers!' I mirrored his facial expression, with my surprise gone but still unable to contribute anything more to the conversation. He was already rising to his feet as I spoke. With a farewell nod he turned and headed back across the grass.

As kind as his offer was, I wouldn't be accepting – no matter how rough the weather might get. Firstly, I was confident that my tent would withstand anything Dartmoor could throw at me. Secondly, I wouldn't feel comfortable sharing a tent with a couple of strangers. Thirdly, and most importantly, I've always thought there is something quite comforting about lying in your tent during inclement weather, listening to the patter of raindrops, conscious of the fact that two sheets of polyester are all that separates you from the elements.

In any event, sunlight now adorned the field once again, without an ominous cloud in sight. The shadows of the camper vans and trees had begun to lengthen as the evening had drawn in.

I dined on a dinner of hot dogs and ketchup, accompanied by a couple of cans of cider that I'd wedged in the shallows of the river to cool.

I decided that tomorrow would be a day of complete rest. In fact, I wouldn't even leave the campsite. Wheal Betsy was one of only two nearby attractions that appealed to me. The other was Brent Tor, with its accompanying church, topping a hill a couple of miles to the west.

The blisters on my feet and toes had grown since yesterday, and I was mindful of the fact that, including my trip along the coast, I still had nearly three weeks of walking planned before my intended return home.

Brent Tor would have to wait until next time. For this, my virgin tour of Dartmoor, my distant view of it from Cudliptown Down would have to do.

I cracked open my second can of cider, and before the day was done I added another simple pleasure to the list of others I'd enjoyed during my respite here; after existing in a state of suspended animation for a whole week, my bowels finally re-awakened.

The next morning, following another long lie-in, I made use of the campsite launderette, before heading for the 'information room' opposite the shop, where I charged my camera batteries and watched a little daytime TV. I also flicked through a stack of leaflets and tourism brochures. Most of them detailed various family-friendly activities across South Devon and a little further afield. Oddly, though, there seemed to be little promotion of the moorlands.

The weather forecast had predicted a day of thundery showers, but at Harford Bridge, the morning had refused to comply, instead developing into another blue-skied scorcher.

I retreated to the shady banks of the river in the afternoon, following the little path through the trees at the edge of the field. Other than the occasional ripple where the current tussled with a boulder here and there, beneath the thick canopy of trees the water appeared as a ribbon of tranquillity. I wondered if I could walk along the shallow edge of the riverbed, down to the pebble beach I'd seen whilst crossing the bridge...?

I took a few cautious steps into the river. Water began to seep into my boots. Then slippery bedrock replaced the subsiding gravel. On my next step I skidded and almost fell.

I decided against that idea.

Instead, I followed the treeline along the field-edge. Near the bridge, the trees gave way to tall, thick swathes of cow parsley, through which another faint path led down to the beach where I'd seen those boys playing with their nets. A wonderfully secluded spot, the beach extended halfway across the water, and partway into one of the three arches of the bridge. Just beyond the beach, a row of small boulders partitioned a deeper, narrower stretch of the river from the shallows.

After filming a panoramic video, I put away my camera gear and knelt down at the edge of the river, examining the patterns of sunlit pebbles – the image of which refracted beneath the shimmering water like a melting oil painting. Shoals of tiny black fish scuttled about below the surface, absorbing the sun's warmth.

I dipped my hands into the water, sending the fish scattering. The cool, gentle current teased through my fingers and lapped seductively at my wrists – contrasting with the subtle itch that had begun to creep over my sunburnt skin over the past 24 hours. I scrunched my palms through the riverbed. A plume of grey sediment swirled up from beneath, temporarily blotting out the pebble-painting.

I'd never been tempted to venture into wild water – mainly because I was unsure as to whether or not I could actually swim. I realise that statement may sound a little odd. I'll explain…

I never learned to swim as a child. Lessons at school were voluntary and I was too shy to participate. My mum had a fear of water so had never learned to swim either – so there was no way she would force me to do so. So, when my brother took me on my first overseas holiday to Thailand in 2002, in my early twenties, he decided it was high time I learned. Of course, *he* had taught *himself* to swim – and boldly declared that I would learn under his tutelage.

As it turned out, his 'lessons' were of a somewhat un-sympathetic nature, generally consisting of him repeatedly pushing me over in the rooftop pool of our hotel in Bangkok, until I started flapping my arms and legs about in a rather ungraceful interpretation of the breaststroke. Eventually, after quite a few dunkings, I mastered the ability to propel myself from one side of the pool to the other. After we'd moved on to the beautiful island of Koh Samui, those lessons translated into the sea, and before returning home a few weeks later, I could manoeuvre about 20 feet through the water.

However, those meagre efforts in the Gulf of Thailand turned out to be my first and last efforts towards becoming a proficient swimmer. In keeping with my habitual indifference regarding exercise, I had stayed out of the water ever since, possessing no desire to follow up those lessons.

Until now.

It was impossible to judge the depth of the river mid-stream, though it couldn't have been more than 25 feet wide. I removed my boots and socks, zipped off the lower legs of my trousers, and stepped into the water.

Once my feet had acclimatised to the temperature, I picked my way across the riverbed, negotiating its loose pebbles and slabs of rock, each step judged with meticulous precision. The water crept above my knees, then tickled at the insides of my thighs. I reached the middle of the river and paused to look up at the bridge – the only place where I might spot any mocking eyes. All that caught my eye was the reflected sunlight dancing on the underside of the bridge's arches.

With the coast clear, I pulled off my tee-shirt and flung it onto the beach. After standing motionless for a few minutes I crouched down, allowing the water to gush up my shorts. This prompted a shudder, followed by an involuntary schoolboy giggle as bubbles floated up around me. The water covered my rotund belly now, skimming an inch or two below my nipples (which, true to form, were protruding from my chest like a couple of pink press-studs).

I remained in this position for a few minutes, bobbing up and down to condition myself to the temperature and assess the current, in anticipation of discovering whether or not I still possessed those aquatic skills I had acquired some 14 years earlier.

Those tiny fish now fluttered by my legs. The stripes running along their sleek bodies faded away into miniscule dorsal fins. The piercing pinpricks of their eyes defined their jittery movements; eerily lifeless, yet apparently engrossed with the mass of pink and white flesh that had invaded their habitat.

I began to practise my arm movements in preparation of a breaststroke attempt. This sent the alien-eyed fish scattering again. But the riverbed was becoming too grating on my tender feet. I stood up and took a step forward, shifting most of my weight onto my heels to relieve my soles. Just as I was contemplating whether to get back down and finally attempt a swim, the pebbles beneath my right heel gave way. With my balance already compromised, the result was inevitable.

I hit the river backwards with a muted splash. My head dunked beneath the water then re-surfaced to flashes of trees and sky as I gasped and snorted. My glasses hung limply from the tip of my nose, splitting and refracting the vision of my flailing feet. My fingers scratched at the riverbed, but could only scrape over loose, slippery stones as I began to drift downstream. Then my hands found a large boulder, covered in some coarse plant-matter, and my drifting body came to a halt. I looked to the steep riverbank a few feet away to my right. Pushing with all my might, I propelled myself to within its reach, grappling at the smooth rocks above the water line. But I couldn't maintain a grip. Finally I managed to seize a tree root, and I pulled myself up against the cliff-like wall of rock and earth.

At that instant I was transported back to that rooftop pool in Bangkok. All I needed was a cackling sibling observing from the riverbank, and this little run of the gauntlet down memory lane would be complete.

With my upper body secured, I forced my feet down to the riverbed. Finding a foothold, I pulled myself upright. Once convinced I wasn't going to topple over, I let go of the root with one hand and adjusted my glasses. I studied the bridge again, half-expecting to see an audience of amused onlookers gawping down at me. Thankfully there was no-one there.

I'd drifted only a few metres from where I'd fallen, but even though I now stood right up against the almost-vertical riverbank, the water still reached my waist. With my hands refusing to surrender the convenient nooks and crannies of the riverbank, I hobbled across the rocky bed, picking my way upstream. Something slimy and repulsive, like the rotting limbs of dead animals, stroked at my legs and ankles with nearly every step.

Eventually I drew level with my tee-shirt back on the beach. More cautiously than ever, I forced myself to let go of the bank and tottered across the shallows. A few years had passed...but eventually my feet touched the sun-baked pebbles once more.

I wrung out my shorts as best I could without taking them off, then plopped down onto the beach. My arms were pockmarked with goose pimples. My entire body trembled. Partly from the cold water. Partly from the adrenaline – yet I felt like howling with laughter.

On reflection, I decided I would not be counting this incident as a fair test of my swimming capabilities; those pebbles had conspired to take me down. Had it not been for them this venture may well have turned out differently. Nevertheless, on the balance of probability, I would still have to answer 'no' to the question of whether or not I could swim. For the time being, anyway.

The sun still blazed down gloriously, though, and my shivers soon subsided. Once my torso was almost dry, I returned myself to a full state of dress, then headed back to the tent.

I had seen no signs of life near any of the recreational vehicles as I'd headed down to the river. However, as I passed by one of the camper vans, I couldn't help noticing an attractive, middle-aged woman sprawled out on the grass, absorbed in a book. Her tight-fitting white tee-shirt was tucked into matching shorts, which, also tight, accentuated her pale but toned thighs. As I passed by she glanced up at me, sending her frizzy blonde hair bouncing around her head.

I was busted. I shot her an apologetic smile and immediately looked away.

'Have you been for a swim, then?' she called out after me. I paused and turned around. She'd propped herself up onto an elbow, her head cocked slightly to one side, with her other arm raised to her forehead to shield her piercing blue eyes from the sun. Her pretty face, pale but equally as smooth and blemish-free as her legs, carried an enlightened smile. I guessed her age as mid-forties. For a split-second I envisioned my pert nipples protruding through my damp tee-shirt. Even before that, though, I'd sensed the rapidly increasing warmth of my flushed cheeks. Now they were practically on fire. I nodded in acknowledgement.

'Kind of, yeah...' I replied, sheepishly returning her smile. Resistance was futile. She could glean whatever information she wanted from me.

'Deeper than it looks, isn't it? I went for a dip myself yesterday.'

I couldn't decide whether this admission was borne of mockery or empathy. I was defenceless either way.

'Yeah...not exactly *Deliverance*...but I think I'll bring my rubber ring next time...' With minimal effort she'd charmed a confession from me.

She responded with a sexy laugh. Whether or not she'd intended it that way was another matter. But that comment was all I could manage before my social inadequacy around beautiful women began to take hold. I shot her a farewell smile, then turned and strolled back to my tent – as excited as I was embarrassed.

The tent had become like a sauna. I stripped off and spread my damp shorts out to dry, then put on some of the fresh clothes I'd laundered that morning. Back outside, I sprawled out in the shadow of the tree, imagining various extensions to my conversation with the alabaster-skinned beauty from across the field.

A little while later I popped up to the shop. Upon returning with a can of chunky sausage and vegetable soup, I discovered I had visitors. The geese and ducks that normally resided up by the reception had paraded down here to rummage in the long grass by my tent. I grabbed my camera and snapped on the zoom lens; this scene would provide some ideal footage for my video diary, serving as something of a metaphor for my relaxing interlude at the campsite.

I lay on my belly so I could shoot from the birds' eyeline, managing to secure a few minutes of footage before they turned camera-shy. Perhaps picking up the scent of a few stale crumbs of bacon sandwiches, the geese then headed straight for my tent. Before I could leap up to shoo them away, they thought better of it and waddled off to the other side of the field.

I hacked at the tin of soup with the can-opener attachment of my knife. It was a laborious task; the tool would cut through the metal only a few millimetres at a time.

As I forced steel through steel I couldn't resist looking casually across the field at the campervan that housed my gorgeous neighbour, but all I saw was steam rising above her windbreaker. Perhaps she was preparing dinner. Would Madame be requiring a dining companion for the evening? Perhaps followed by a romantic dip in the river by moonlight…preferably without her date nearly drowning…?

Suddenly a mass of curly dark hair popped up over the windbreaker. My girl had company.

Following that crushing realisation, I dispelled the last shred of my half-baked romantic notions, and returned my attention to my can opening. The steel buckled as I forced my tool through it more vigorously. Moments later the lid snapped up and spat specks of brown soup into my face.

This would be the last dinner of my hike in surroundings such as these. It was a moment to savour. But although my batteries (and not just those for my camera) had been thoroughly re-charged, I was eager to get back onto the moor and resume my adventure.

As tiny bubbles began to surface from the depths of the saucepan, I wiped those flecks of soup from my face, cracked open my last can of cider, and raised a toast.

'To the Harford Bridge Campsite. And to romance…'

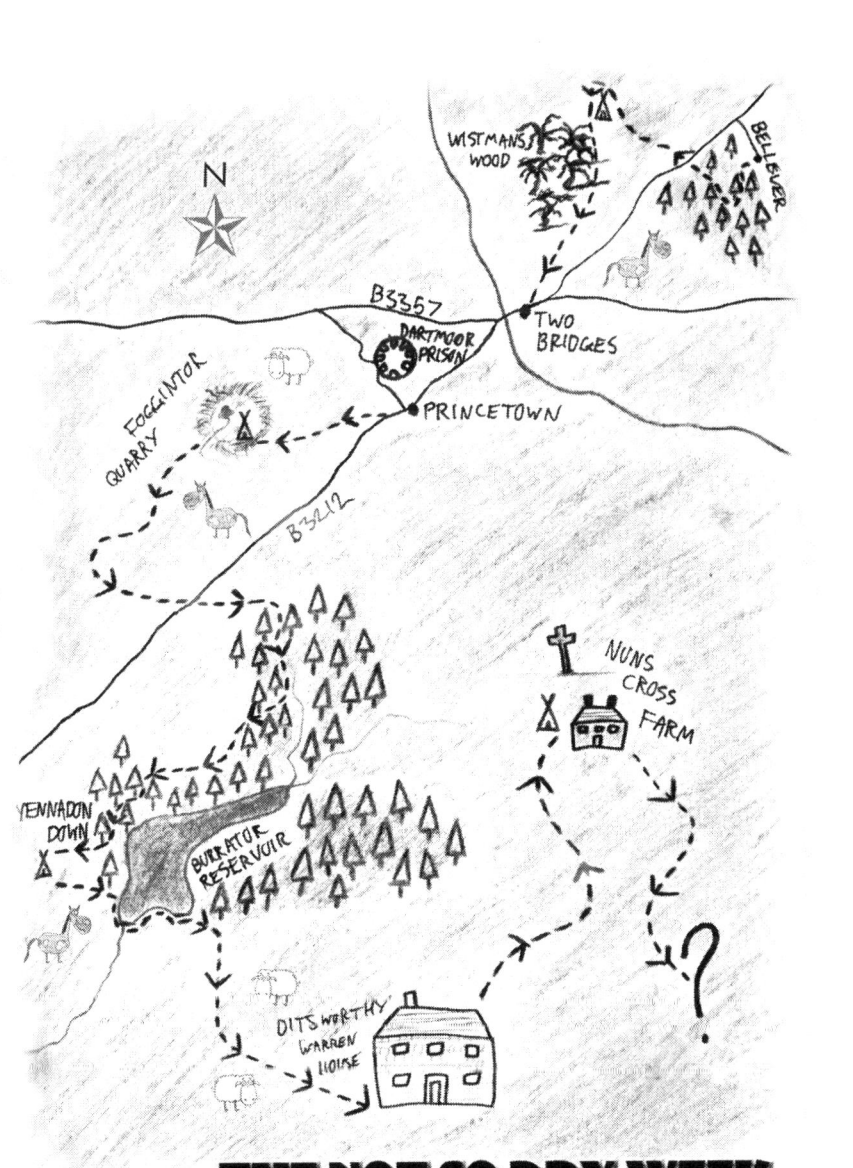

THE NOT SO DRY WEEK

Chapter Six: Close Encounters

Harford Bridge Campsite to Wistman's Wood

Despite my sunburn I had no right to complain about the weather I'd been afforded so far on this hike. I felt like I could almost count the number of raindrops that had touched my skin. But as my ninth day on Dartmoor dawned, my luck finally ran out; a rhythmic crackling on the flysheet underscored my awakening.

I unzipped the tent and surveyed the field. The grey rectangle of barbecued grass had turned to mush. The young couple nearby had packed up and gone. For once, my friendly neighbour who had offered me shelter from the elements was absent from his awning. A man donning a red poncho was returning from the taps, swinging a bottle of water from each hand. Above, a few specks of blue sky poked through menacing, sultry clouds. I recalled yesterday's weather forecasts, reminding me how parts of Dartmoor had seen thunderstorms. No doubt my turn for a drenching was still to come – and would quite possibly come today.

Soon I would be leaving the campsite, heading south-east to the tiny village of Bellever, almost right in the centre of the national park. From there I would hike south-west through forest, before rejoining the moors and ascending between two tors, eventually camping in an area about a mile north-west of a place called Wistman's Wood.

In a break from hiking protocol, I would be taking a bus – two buses, to be exact – first to the small town of Tavistock, then another to Bellever. This had always been my intention, rain or shine, rather than waste a day's walk along the busy B3357, covering ground I'd already passed through.

I rummaged through my pack for my waterproof jacket and trousers. These garments were old and tired, having toured the UK with me over the years – most notably in Snowdonia, where they had failed spectacularly to keep me dry. I attributed this to the fact that I hadn't bothered to re-spray them with any waterproof coating since their previous use. Or the one before that. Or ever, in fact. I had assumed, perhaps arrogantly, that this recommendation was simply a scare tactic cooked up by the manufacturers of the garments and the spray, in cahoots together to get us naïve shoppers to part with more cash. Defiantly stepping out into the deluge like some smart-arse consumer champion and a paragon of virtue, I was determined to prove those sprays were a waste of money. Half an hour later I was trudging back to my tent soaked to the skin. Lesson learned.

Subsequently, I always made sure I gave those layers a re-coat before packing them for any excursion. They had performed adequately since that week in Snowdonia – although they had yet to be tested in any torrent on a par with the downpours of *that* holiday. The closest simulation I could get was to stand in the bath and pour jugs of water over myself. Not a drop breached the polyester. That was sufficient to convince me they were impenetrable.

After breakfast, I showered and restored my goatee beard to its proper definition, then departed from the campsite at about 10:00am, pausing on my way out to double-check the location of the bus stop with the lady at reception.

As his estate car trundled over the speed bumps along the driveway, the man who'd offered to put me up in his awning waved farewell – still with that canny expression fixed on his face. I responded in kind, then got moving.

As I crossed Harford Bridge and trudged up the hill towards the bus stop, with my full ensemble strapped to my back for the first time in days, I realised those cushy few days had allowed me to become a little complacent regarding the rigours of my hike. I told myself to think of the health benefits. Aside from taking a long bath, my first task, when I eventually got home in a couple of weeks, would be to weigh myself...

Arriving at a crossroads, huffing and puffing, I glanced up at a rusty iron signpost. Its white paint was flaking off even more severely than the skin of my nose. The words 'Peter Tavy Cross' were embossed along the top, as was each destination upon its four pointers. I remembered this location from my research into the few bus services I'd need during my hike. However, although this location was marked on the map, the post itself wasn't actually marked as a bus stop. I put this down to the simple assumption that out here in the sticks, the task of providing clear bus stop signage probably wasn't top of the agenda for the local council. Besides, I'd checked with the woman at the campsite that this was definitely the right place to catch the bus. So, as the rain crackled against my waterproofs, I waited patiently for my ride.

Five minutes passed. The bus was now late.

A trickle of sweat wriggled down the small of my back.

After ten minutes I began to wonder if I was in the wrong place.

I hung around indecisively, watching as a couple of guys on mountain bikes, dressed like giant insects in their neon lycra, effortlessly ascended the hill that had nearly broken me. They were heading towards the village of Peter Tavy – which I now suspected to be the true location of the fabled bus stop – about a mile away. Despite their exertion they still carried enough air in their lungs to offer an enthusiastic greeting as they passed. I reciprocated, then watched their powerful calf muscles contort as they peddled away.

As their lurid bodies disappeared around a bend, I set off after them.

An hour or so after leaving the campsite I arrived back at its reception, having wasted that entire time walking into Peter Tavy and scouring the village for a bus stop. I'd asked the one person I'd seen – an elderly chap washing his car – if he knew of its whereabouts. He'd looked at me as if I'd asked him to explain Einstein's Theory of General Relativity – before reliably informing me that no buses ever passed through this village.

Back at the campsite, I sweated profusely beneath my unbreathable waterproofs, whilst beads of rain clung to their exterior. I waited behind a customer in the shop, itching to interrogate the woman again. Relying on such a scant timetable, missing the next bus would mean a disastrous teatime arrival at Bellever.

The customer left and I repeated my earlier enquiry. She repeated her instructions – this time throwing in a few hand-gestures to assert her authority on the subject. I left. Again. And followed her directions. Again. But this time there was one principal difference: she told me to turn *left* outside the campsite. I swear to this day she'd told me to go *right* the first time. She'd also told me it was five minutes away. Now it was ten.

As it turned out it was more like 20 minutes, but soon enough I was standing beneath a vivid, orange and green bus-stop sign, complete with a shiny timetable entitled Peter Tavy Cross – despite the fact that I was standing nowhere near the village of Peter Tavy. Or the actual location on the map that shared that name. Anyway, even brighter than that sign was the waterproof cover of my pack, so there was no danger of the driver not seeing me when the bus came rolling along the road minutes later.

I boarded, paid my fare and took a seat near the front. A few elderly couples occupied the middle rows of seats. They paid little attention to my joining them – whilst a couple of teenagers at the back openly gawped at me as I performed my pack-removing ritual.

I arrived in Tavistock just in time to catch the second bus, which was filled almost to capacity as it pulled out of the tiny station. This journey was the more pleasant of the two, as the road headed out of town and joined the B3357, weaving east through a collage of yellows and browns, returning me to the heart of Dartmoor.

After a while the road merged with the B3212. Thereafter the bus cruised alongside a coniferous woodland, by which point myself and a silver-haired old lady were the only remaining passengers. Then the bus turned off onto a narrow lane before reaching its final stop in Bellever, where the old lady stood up to depart. As I got up to follow her, the driver told me he could drop me off round the corner at the youth hostel if I preferred. I accepted the offer, flattered by his assumption that I was young enough to be staying at a youth hostel.

With a bone-snapping crunch of gravel, the bus pulled away from the turnout, its engine rumbling confidently as it shifted up a gear. The rain had passed and the clouds had thinned a little, but the sun still struggled to make an appearance amidst the muggy air.

Going by the timetable at the bus stop I deduced that the time must have been a little after 2:00pm. I was about an hour behind schedule.

After watching the bus chug back up the lane, I glanced around Bellever. How could this place ever have been designated a village? I could count the buildings on one hand; a few tiny houses dominated by the youth hostel, with its contemporary, geometric roof poking above the treetops, distinguishing the structure from the neighbouring post-war houses. I had envisaged groups of youngsters assembling outside the place, perhaps preparing for fishing or orienteering trips, but aside from a couple of parked cars, the forecourt was deserted.

Behind me, heading south, a four-wheel-drive track disappeared into the pinewoods beyond a gate, which bore a sign declaring this route for Forestry Commission-use only. But I wasn't heading that way. After consulting my map and compass I headed south-west, climbing a steep bridleway that ran alongside, and frequently merged with, a shallow stream.

My stomach began to growl as I ascended, taking care not to slip on the wet path. My hunger shouldn't have been a surprise; I'd eaten my breakfast about six hours ago. But, of course, during my hike I'd grown accustomed to a suppressed appetite. Perhaps my poo at the campsite had jolted my metabolism back into some semblance of normality?

Once the gradient had levelled off almost flat, I stopped for a bite to eat. With my chocolate bars gone and my biscuits rationed, I'd have to prepare some couscous. Thankfully, having not touched the stuff for a good few days, my aversion to it had waned. I set up my stove at one end of a damp wooden bench overlooking the village, and whilst waiting for my water to boil I assessed the views.

By my reckoning, I'd climbed 50 metres or so up into Bellever Forest – though I lacked the inclination to check the contour lines on the map to confirm this. To the left, coniferous trees dominated the near landscape, replaced in the distance by the ever-present, pale patchwork of moorland fading into the haze. A gap in the trees closer to me revealed a farmhouse and a trio of horses roaming a field. The nearby stream, over ages, had gouged out a huge chunk of the hillside, roughly marking my route up from the village. In the mid-distance, the B3212 stretched onward to the horizon, carrying sparse traffic to the eastern side of the national park.

Silent traffic.

Finally, I was returning to the wilds of Dartmoor.

Soon after setting off again following that impromptu lunchbreak, the hill levelled off completely and the trees thinned. Then I came to a crossroads, which presented me with my first sighting of Bellever Tor, about a kilometre away. From this distance, these rocks bore a slight resemblance to the mighty Great Links Tor, in the sense that they appeared to consist of layers of flat rocks piled on top of each other, squashed into those fat cookie shapes. I'd initially intended to pay a visit to this feature, but being behind schedule, and factoring in my tally of visited tors, I decided to pass on this one, opting instead for a wide shot of it beneath the moody clouds.

Soon I was back in dense forest. The path narrowed and massive conifers towered over me on either side, maybe 20 metres high, with great mounds of thick, mossy vegetation carpeting the earth between them. Fallen trees lined – and occasionally blocked – the path, forcing me to either clamber over or detour around them. The tempestuous sky had been punctured again, but I was so hot beneath my waterproofs that the prospect of a little rain on my skin had become rather appealing. I'd also grown tired of their rustling, which evoked the sensation of being dressed in bin liners. So off they came.

I reached another crossroads and turned right. This new path would eventually lead me out of the forest before crossing the B3212, heading back into more familiar terrain. An increasing presence, though, and clearly delighted by my sweaty, pale skin, were my old friends, the midges. At first I ignored them, but as I paused to take a photo of the massive tree trunks, they descended in hordes to feast on my arms and face. I swished at them between adjustments of camera settings – then remembered that I'd bought some midge repellent at the campsite.

I took off my pack and fished out the canister. The hiss of the spray appeared to panic the critters as I coated my arms liberally. I then engaged in an all-out attack, attempting to take out anything flying within a few feet. I shut my eyes and sprayed the stuff around my head. Its acrid stench scuttled along my nasal passages and into my throat. A layer of bitter chemicals deposited over my tonsils, which attempted to expel them in a hacking cough. The vile taste spared me after a few seconds and I took a hefty swig of water. Still the insects swarmed around me to some extent…but appeared to have learned their lesson.

Once I'd bagged my desired shot of the trees I continued on my route, shortly emerging from the forest to cross the road along which the bus had brought me. Even though not a single tree lay ahead of me anymore, officially I still stood within the county parish of Dartmoor Forest. Geographically speaking, this was the largest parish in the whole of Devon – yet at the last count, its population stood at a mere 1,619.

Well, that night it would be 1,620. My intended campsite lay just over the hills ahead, about two miles to the west as the crow flies – but probably closer to three along the dotted green line of the path that meandered across the map.

Along this route I would pass by Wistman's Wood – a famed patch of ancient woodland nestled on the banks of the West Dart River, made up of a tangled mass of stunted oak trees that, over centuries, had twisted themselves into bizarre contortions. Only a handful of truly ancient woodlands remain across the British countryside, and this would be my first visit to any of them.

Like much of Dartmoor, Wistman's Wood has been the subject of various legends and ghost stories over the years. The most notable of these are those associated with the Druids; they practised pagan rituals at the site, and the corpses of their dead were carried through the wood in procession before being buried in the village of Lydford, nearly ten miles away. These funeral cortèges have been attributed to reports of ghostly apparitions seen around the edges of the wood. Other legends abound include that of the Wisht Hounds – a pack of huge, ravenous black dogs with red eyes and massive yellow fangs. These beasts would hide amongst knotted tree roots and boulders by day, emerging after nightfall to stalk the moor for weary travellers and unbaptised children. Any unfortunate soul to cross their paths would be dragged back to their dens and torn to pieces. The hounds are said to be commanded by the Devil himself, or by an ancient spirit known as Old Crockern, who lives nearby on the aptly named Crockern Tor.

It was these stories that made Wistman's Wood one of the most enticing locations of my entire hike. Initially I'd considered camping there. Annoyingly, though, the wood was situated outside of those permitted camping areas – the wild camper real estate of Dartmoor. I'd therefore selected an alternative location about a kilometre away. Of course, the ghost stories had nothing to do with that decision…

The wood was marked on the map by a tiny green splodge,

covering no more than a few hundred square-metres. The path along which I was about to continue passed quite close to it, so I didn't anticipate any problems seeking out the place. But as I had begun to realise, following footpaths on Dartmoor wasn't always as straightforward as one might think.

I passed through a gate at the roadside and headed for the hills.

A majestic beast, with a creamy white coat and a windswept, blonde mane, stood at the far end of the field from where I'd crossed another gate. I first assumed it was another Dartmoor Pony – but then surely such an animal wouldn't be out here all by itself? He was also a little on the large side for a pony, standing like a reluctant sentry and eyeing me with only a fleeting interest. Virtually every equine I'd encountered over the past nine days had been a vivacious creature, frolicking without a care in the world within their social groups. Here before me now stood this introverted loner. All things considered, this animal had to be a horse. Horse or pony, though, he appeared to be in need of cheering up. Perhaps having his photo taken would do the trick?

About half a dozen metres away, I paused to get out my camera gear. After snapping on my 35mm lens (a perfect choice for portraits) I cautiously made my approach.

I had assumed the animal was a male – but nothing about its physique suggested that assumption was correct. However, although I can't claim to be an expert on sexing *any* creature (not even humans, based on another incident of my Thailand holiday, but that is a whole other story…), I'd been led to believe most mammals are highly proficient at concealing their genitalia. This I'd learned not only from David Attenborough, but also from the surprise reaction that greeted me one time when I tickled the belly of Jasper – my mum's now dearly-departed mongrel. Something told me I would not be sexing *this* animal by any similar means, though.

Every few steps closer I got, the equine gave a subtle reaction: a slight turn of the head…a shuffle of the hooves…a swish of the tail.

Once or twice, from between a few wayward locks of his mane and his thick blonde lashes, his eyes briefly met mine. Each nuance of behaviour instructed me to pause for a few seconds, until I was confident that he wasn't going to either trot away or deliver a belting kick to my head. I'd greeted horses on several occasions since the 'Horse-Humper' incident of my childhood, but never without the reassuring presence of a fence or gate between us.

Once I was within touching distance, I paused one last time, then raised my hand to his face. He turned his head, revealing details of the wispy beard trailing from his jaw. He swished his tail again as I waited for him to be still once more...as still as I was...rooted to the spot, my pulse quickening. That moment of stillness arrived a few seconds later. After a few more his eyes fixed on mine. I raised my hand towards his neck. My fingertips met his thin coat, then traced the subtle definition of muscle beneath, tussling through locks of his bedraggled mane, as if I were pulling apart candyfloss. His nostrils wavered as he sniffed the air. I moved my hand towards his nose, but he turned away, this time with a snort.

That was enough for me.

I stepped back to take my photo, hoping he would really indulge me and look straight into the camera. But those partially-concealed eyes had lost whatever shred of interest they displayed moments ago. I tried to garner his attention with a few cliché horse impressions, sinking to a rather pathetic whinny in desperation. I tried moving in front of him, but still he refused to pose. Judging by the return of his shuffling body language, his patience was waning.

I settled for a shot of him in profile, then bid him farewell.

The path led me to an assortment of abandoned stone buildings, covered in moss and lichen. Some had been sunk into the ground by a few feet, without a roof or door remaining on any of them. As wind whistled through the gaps in the metre-thick walls, I entered one of the rooms.

These buildings had been part of a gunpowder mill, operational from 1844 to 1896, and gifting the name of 'Powdermills' to a nearby pottery. Until the invention of dynamite in 1867, gunpowder was used extensively across Dartmoor, mainly for quarrying and tin mining. The buildings comprising these works had purposely been built with flimsy, light roofing, to minimise casualties in the event of any explosions – the theory being that the roof would be blown outwards rather than collapsing in on the workers. The same logic accounted for the walls having been built so thick – although, according to the history books, this had proved insufficient to prevent all tragedies. Like the moorland near Okehampton, this area had also been used as a training ground for around 3,000 American troops prior to the D-Day landings. Of course, by that time the site had long since been closed down, and not an ounce of its deadly black powder remained.

A foreboding growl of thunder suddenly assuaged the whistling wind. A dark, bulging mass of cloud had swept in overhead, filling the entire rectangle of sky visible from within the derelict building. I hurried back outside, where the cloud's full form crudely resembled an upturned pyramid. I expected another thunderclap to announce an imminent downpour at any second. But it never came.

I continued with my exploration. The most striking of the structures were two huge chimneys, situated a couple of hundred metres apart, standing about as high as Wheal Betsy and about ten feet wide. A closer inspection of one of them revealed a hole at the base, into which a child – or perhaps a diminutive adult – could crawl. I had no intention, however, of finding out if I could fit through there (diminutive is not a word anyone would use to describe my physique...).

The nearby Powdermills Pottery also featured a museum, which would have been worth adding to my itinerary had I been a pottery enthusiast. I am not – so I continued along the path as it passed by the pottery's perimeter and beyond the chimneys, before turning away further west.

The stormy clouds had dissipated, but a light rain began to fall again as I left the pottery behind. I put my jacket back on…only to remove it soon after, still preferring a cool drizzle on my skin to being drenched in sweat as I ascended the hill towards Longaford Tor. Each time I glanced back to gauge my progress, those chimneys took a little longer to identify. The higher I climbed the same became true of the path ahead, until it became no longer distinguishable at all. Then Longaford Tor also disappeared. I hoped one of the two would soon return – otherwise I would be navigating with only my map and compass.

After a while I reached a drystone wall, high enough to prevent my peering over it. I was supposed to cross this en route to Longaford Tor. However, the absence of any stile or gate confirmed that somewhere along the way I must have strayed from the path. According to the map, the correct route crossed the wall not far from a point where it formed a tee-junction with another that ran down the hill…but there were no other walls in sight. My instincts told me to go right, and shortly after a grey line appeared above the grass tussocks. That line soon became a wall…then a junction of them. Then I reached a stile.

Its wet, wooden planks creaked beneath the combined weight of myself and my pack as I gripped the side-struts, heaving myself up as the wind and rain beat against my clothes. At the top, two clusters of rocks appeared in the distance; Longaford Tor. Immediately behind them lay the valley of the West Dart River.

After clambering down the other side I pushed on towards the tor – although it had disappeared from view as soon as I'd stepped down from the stile. Briefly, at least, the path regained a little definition. Then the two rock formations re-appeared and the gradient eased. Finally I reached the top of the hill, where, between the clusters of rocks, I took off my pack to take a break.

The boulders forming the tor lacked any obvious route to the top – to the extent that I didn't possess the nerve to try scaling them for a more extensive view of the valley below.

There was something rather Martian about these surroundings; something I hadn't sensed at the ridges of the hills I'd climbed previously. If I could have swapped the grey sky for a red one, and have some kind of moon-buggy crawl out from behind the rocks, I could have easily believed that a wormhole had sucked me in and transported me to the red planet. I could have been a modern-day, slightly more sci-fi version of *Dorothy Gale* – only lacking in the frilly dress department and not quite as camp (but pretty close, some might argue). Perhaps somewhere beneath these rocks I would find a pair of magic walking boots, dangling from the feet of the *Wicked Campsite Receptionist of the West*...

Of greater significance than the Martian landscape, though, was the fact that having reached the ridge of the hill, there was no sign yet of Wistman's Wood. It should have now been only half a kilometre away to the south-west. I strolled across the ridge, somewhat confused by the absence of anything in sight that would equate to that green splodge on the map. To the right lay nothing but desolate hills, broken up only by a faint, jagged line marking the narrowest stretch of the West Dart River, disappearing at its source. To the left, the river had cut a deeper scar, dominating the view downstream (it is widely believed that rivers once flowed on Mars, too...), though the river itself remained hidden amongst thick shrubs at the bottom of the valley.

I had little doubt as to my bearings; the river and the tor pinpointed my exact location – so where was Wistman's Wood? Then I reminded myself that as much as I wanted to explore that wood, right at that moment, finding the path was of greater importance. Without it, I would be unable to find my camping location. My plan had initially been to visit the wood, then cross the river and climb the other side of the valley to my next camping spot. Being behind schedule, though, I would have to camp first and possibly postpone my visit to the wood until the morning.

A faint, dark line ran down the hillside – the resumption of the path, surely? I attempted to trace its route to where it would cross the river, but the line disappeared amongst the heathland way short of the riverbank. The line re-appeared on the other side of the valley, running from a grey, un-natural bulge over the river. A weir. Surely I could cross there? However, a map-check revealed the line to be another leat, with no path marked alongside it – and flowing away from my intended camping spot.

I then took a moment to pause my geographical quandary, clearing my mind to take in the wild, mercurial beauty around me. With the rocky ridge lit up by the rising sun, a fantastic sunrise photo could be on offer from up here. Perhaps with more of the swirling mist that had swept across Walkhampton Common. Strictly speaking, I was now in an area where camping was prohibited – but I refused to let this issue interfere with my Dartmoor adventure any longer. Besides, the chances of my being able to camp at my intended location were beginning to slip away.

I scratched around the tor in search of a patch of grass big enough to house me – but even with my modest tent, this proved fruitless. I wrestled my pack onto my shoulders and set off, hoping to find a pitch further down the hillside.

As the valley turned from grey to green, the rougher and mushier the terrain became as I lost the path yet again. Even whilst bypassing the sloppiest areas, my progress became tediously slow. Then the midges returned. These were a tougher tribe, too – apparently immune to the spray that had afforded me some respite from them earlier. Then, some distance away to my left, a dark clump of trees emerged from the bracken: Wistman's Wood.

I was *not* going any further. I would camp here and then go ghost hunting in the wood by the eerie light of dusk. But my issue of finding precisely where to pitch remained. Rocks, reeds, tussocks, rabbit holes or mud-pits covered virtually every square inch of this area. But as the sky slowly darkened and the rain began to fall heavier, my pitch-eligibility criteria became less discriminating – even less so when the growl of thunder returned. I picked out a spot that would just about do and up went the tent.

Having been forced to pack the thing away in the rain that morning, the inside was quite damp. At least my sleeping bag had remained bone-dry inside my pack, as had my mat, inside its polythene bag. After unrolling them both, I lay down and listened to the rhythmic patter of the rain, along with an occasional rumble. Soon the patter became a rattling. Then a hammering. Not to be outdone, the thunderclaps also became angrier and more frequent.

The thunderstorm continued for a while, but by the time the local radio station had broadcast its 8:00pm news bulletin, the clatter had almost ceased, although the weather forecast informed me that I should expect rain throughout the night.

Normally by this time I would have been preparing my saucepan of rice, but following my unusual lunch break earlier, I had barely any appetite. I was also low on water – but couldn't be persuaded to go back outside to try and find a route down to the river.

Ketchup!

Crammed into one of the side pockets of my pack was the bottle of ketchup I'd bought at the campsite, still about a third full. I teased it out and squeezed its contents into my gaping mouth. Mouthfuls of the sweet, tangy sauce slid down my throat; a refreshing alternative to what had become my usual fare out on the moors.

Dusk approached with a graceful subtlety – unlike the racket on the tent, which began to beat hard again not long after my skimpy supper, reaching enough decibels even to drown out the radio. I turned up the volume, but this also increased the distortion of the less-than-perfect reception. But was that a sign? Perhaps the sounds of nature were *meant* to automatically trump any noise *I* could make out here. My other, less philosophical, noise-related concern referred to my fears over my (strictly speaking, illegal) encampment.

So I turned the radio off.

Later, the rain had eased and the thunder had moved some distance away. The flashes of lightning preceding each groan were now merely flickers in the twilight. Dense, low cloud smothered the ridges either side of the valley. From this perspective, the spiny plants and grasses around my tent completely concealed Wistman's Wood. Soon, only a monochrome assortment of dark shapes would remain before they too would be consumed by the darkness – leaving the moor at the mercy of the Wisht Hounds. Unless, of course, the volatile sky would convince them to remain in their dens. That seemed unlikely, though…

A resurgent spray of raindrops battered against the flysheet – and my face. I zipped up the tent, then reached for my book and headlamp.

Once night was fully upon me and the rain had eased again, I conducted another survey of the dirty sky. Where might the Moon have been hiding amidst that impenetrable cloud? This scene would have looked stunning beneath the moonlight – from the expanse of the valley and the trees below, right down to the raindrops, which would have gleamed like tiny pearls at the tips of the grasses and reeds.

Given the tendency for mist and cloud to blanket the moor from dusk till dawn, I had yet to observe the Moon over Dartmoor. The only clear night sky I'd been gifted had been that first one by Meldon Reservoir. Although, to be fair to the weather, that was also the only occasion in which I'd shown any real interest in the night sky.

That first night, the Moon was at its new phase, so hadn't been visible at all. Since then it would have risen later each day, with a little more of its crescent visible each night. Now, nine nights later, the Moon would be close to full. But even a brilliant Full Moon would struggle to make an appearance through this cloud. Perhaps the weather would show some clemency over the next few days?

At that thought, a fat raindrop hit my glasses and rolled down the lens, pausing insolently a few times along the way. The droplet contorted my view into something resembling an impressionist painting. It clung to the bottom of the frame for a few seconds then plopped to the ground.

That rogue raindrop marked a fall in their numbers, however; the patter on the tent was fast losing its rhythm. The thunderclaps had given up, too.

Then the rain stopped completely.

I *was* going ghost hunting, after all...

I decided against taking my camera gear with me. Stumbling in the dark and damaging my precious gear was an eventuality I was not prepared to risk. Besides, what were the odds of actually photographing a ghost? Unlikely at best. So, donning my waterproofs and headlamp, I stepped out into the night, carrying nothing but my eager sense of anticipation.

With extreme caution, I picked my way across the hillside in the torchlight, seeking out the area where I'd spotted the trees earlier. Once or twice, I almost lost my footing as my feet sank into the squidgy grass, but soon enough the furthest reaches of the torch beam found a dark mass poking above the tussocks. Then something reached up, clawing through the darkness. Something like long, gnarled fingers, faintly returning a pale blue in the distant torchlight.

The tussocks gave way to bracken. Then I came upon a narrow dirt track, appearing as if it might lead to the edge of the wood. Slippery rocks frequently protruded from the mud, but, maintaining my cautious approach, I soon found myself within a few metres of the trees.

I abandoned the path, stepping precariously down a short but steep bank, edging my way another few metres towards the boulders between the trees, now almost within touching distance. The torch sprayed a film of cyan over everything that escaped its immediate glare. What then greeted me, even in the limited light, or perhaps because of it, was otherworldly.

Forging a path through the rocks, a tangled web of trunk-less boughs and thick branches crawled from the earth, twisting upwards, jostling for space before terminating at the fingertips I'd glimpsed earlier. Like a fungus, moss dripped from them in clumps. The fingertips sprouted nails, entwining in their unstoppable growth and decorated by a thin canopy of leaves. These trees could have been the hands of giants imprisoned beneath the rocks – themselves also smothered by a carpet of moss – although determining which fingers belonged to which hands was impossible. As the torchlight faded into the depths of the wood, my eyes demanded more – but this was all the trees would permit.

Feeling like a character from a Tim Burton movie (and way cooler than Dorothy Gale), I crouched down in front of one of the boulders, where the blazing white light re-enforced the furry, alien quality of the moss. Coarse and cold, touching it imparted on me the bizarre notion that the plant had deposited its spores onto my skin. Would I awaken tomorrow smothered in the same manner as those giant fingers...? I lifted my hand away, smiling in bewilderment.

Suddenly I found myself disapproving of the artificial light cast by the headlamp. The more of the wood I beheld by torchlight, the more inherent the danger was of this diminishing my daylight exploration. So I switched the headlamp off. As impractical as it might be, I wanted to take in Wistman's Wood naturally. With a little luck, maybe the clouds would part, allowing a glimpse of the trees beneath the moonlight.

I remained crouched next to the rocks, motionless, for an eternity, my eyes gradually adjusting to the dark. I expected to hear an owl hooting or the squeaking of a bat...but nothing broke the silence.

Nothing until, some distance away, the faintest rumble of thunder tumbled through the clouds. Rain began to patter on the leaves. Eventually my unaided eyes were able to perceive the outline of the furry rocks and the largest of the tree-limbs.

My toes were beginning to tingle; my feet hadn't moved in ages. I told myself to stand up and get the blood flowing again. But I envisioned my head entangling in the creeping fingernails overhead, the crusty things clawing at my face. I smiled inwardly, then re-engaged my dormant calf muscles. A coldness gushed through my feet as I stood up. Then the blood began to flow freely once more. I wriggled my toes to assist the circulation.

Then something rustled. Behind me. Amidst the patter of the rain. Normally I would have assumed it was a sheep, but I hadn't seen a single one of them around here. Nor any ponies, for that matter (why not...???).

I refused to entertain the notion that somewhere behind me, perhaps just a few metres away, stood a bloodthirsty, drooling canine, slapping its tongue over long, yellow fangs, its evil red eyes sizing up its next meal – devoid of fear or pity for this unyielding, tingly-toed stranger. But despite my rejection of that fantasy, I couldn't bring myself to turn around and switch on my headlamp.

The noise repeated as I stood there, paralysed. My tent was pitched illegally just a few hundred metres away. Was there some farmer out on a night patrol, on the hunt for trespassing wild campers? That seemed unlikely – but slightly more plausible than the possibility that I was being stalked by some ghostly monster.

Dismissing such absurdities, I snapped myself back into reality. Over the years I had encountered various species during my night-photography sessions. Foxes. Badgers... I switched on my headlamp and turned around. With trepidation I studied the blue-tinged, dew-laden clumps of grass adorning the hillside.

There was no animal, or eyes, in sight.

The noise came again. Fainter. Whatever it was, it was going away. The rain, on the other hand, was starting to fall heavily again.

For now, I'd seen enough of Wistman's Wood.

I fumbled my way back up to the path then headed for my camp. Raindrops flashed across my blue-tinted field of vision, but I managed to retrace my steps. Before long, through the deluge, I sighted the unmistakeable outline of the tent.

Back inside my sanctuary I dragged off my waterproofs and tossed them into a corner. I climbed into my sleeping bag, musing over how – momentarily – I had allowed the legends of Wistman's

Wood to get the better of me. I was also glad I had kept my exploration short. Not because of whatever had spooked me out there, and not really because of the weather, but because my short, night-time visit had preserved my anticipation; in the light of the coming dawn I would behold Wistman's Wood in all its glory.

I zipped up my sleeping bag.

After a while, the patter on the tent softened again.

'Let them come...' I whispered, as the rhythmic rain sang me a lullaby.

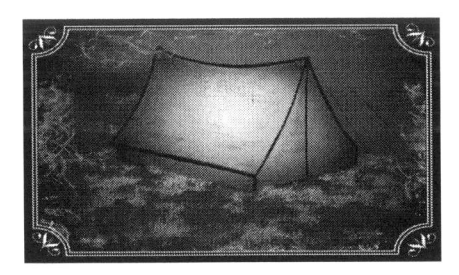

Chapter Seven: Isolation

Wistman's Wood to Foggintor Quarry

Sporadic, thundery showers awakened me throughout the night. On the final such instance I found myself hunched into a foetal position, having slid down the mat again after pitching on sloping ground. My feet felt unusually cold and damp. Alerted to the possibility that water had penetrated the tent, I sat up and reached for the headlamp. The torchlight revealed rain seeping in where my feet had pushed the two layers of polyester onto one another, resulting in a line of tiny pools accumulating along the edge of the groundsheet. I climbed out of my sleeping bag and mopped up with toilet paper (for obvious reasons, this was still in plentiful supply).

I poked my head outside. A hint of colour was creeping over the moorland as dawn approached. Somewhere to my left, beyond the rocks of Longaford Tor, the sun lay close to the horizon. Only the compass needle told me this, though, on account of the uniformly thick cloud that filled the sky.

To some campers, this would have made for a lacklustre start to the day. Indeed, on scrutinising the landscape, I realised my envisioning of a dramatic, misty shot of the valley had been in vain. But I would take what I had been given, and for a photographer about to shoot an ethereal woodland scene, the elements were actually not all that far from perfection.

The *perfect* weather would have been the mist or fog I'd so far witnessed only once in all its glory, as the diffused sunlight would ensure that the trees were evenly lit, whilst also blotting out any distracting background. This would have perfectly matched my photos to the evocative mysteries associated with Wistman's Wood. In the absence of any such mist or fog, though, I would gladly take the overcast sky as a close second.

With the wood just a short walk away, I felt isolated enough to leave my remaining several-hundred-pounds' worth of gear behind, so I headed out with nothing other than my camera and wide-angle lens, my jacket, and an improvised rain cover for my camera: a plastic carrier bag.

As I strode across the hillside, the edge of the wood emerged from a thin haze and a light rain began to fall. I tucked my camera under my jacket and pulled my hood over my head. Soon the rain was pelting down. Through the spray that stippled my glasses, I glanced up at the mass of dark cloud creeping overhead. The flimsy plastic bag would not protect my camera from *this*.

I abandoned my excursion and hurried back to the tent.

Owing to my dwindling water supply, a skimpy breakfast – consisting of a few swigs of water and a couple of biscuits – followed the skimpy supper of the previous evening.

A little over an hour later the rain had ceased, so I pulled my boots back on.

Then I heard voices.

Close enough to reveal snippets of conversation; some nattering on the subject of office politics. The jabbering steadily increased in volume…then faded away.

I waited.

Then, like an ostrich scanning the savannah for predators, I poked my head outside and surveyed the valley. There was no sign of anyone, anywhere.

I waited a few minutes more, then stepped outside again. My earlier sense of isolation had evaporated – so this time I packed up *everything*, then headed for Wistman's Wood for the final time.

One of a few remnants of a vast forest that covered the area many thousands of years ago, no-one really knows quite how old Wistman's Wood is. Following the end of the last Ice Age, deciduous forests thrived across Dartmoor – although the climate remained cool enough to stunt their growth, resulting in the characteristic, gnarled appearance of the trees. Around 5000BC, humans cleared most of the forests, initially to attract game for hunting, then later for agriculture. So why had this little patch of trees been spared? Was it held in high religious regard for some reason? Or had the thick layer of ankle-twisting boulders, from which the wood sprouted, offered some protection from would-be tree-burners? Either way, the presence of numerous Bronze Age remains close to Wistman's Wood confirms that these trees have attracted human beings for millennia – and I was the latest of them to be drawn to this fantastical place.

The clouds remained sympathetic to my photographic requirements, thinning a little but still blocking out any blazing sunlight. I made my way to the ferns, which were now a lush and vivid green as opposed to the washed-out, alien appearance they had returned in the torchlight. Then I found the end of the path, leading me to the wood once more.

In order to make a tangible comparison between night and day, I scanned the trees for the same spot I'd found last night. I soon found a tiny clearing, at the back of which a large rock poked up before a bed of thick branches, weaving amongst one another like masses of furry snakes. This was the place where I had crouched in the dark on my numbed toes.

Wistman's Wood had lost none of its gothic charm in the daylight. But gone were my fears of the Wisht Hounds. Instead, I half-expected Gollum to pop out from behind the rocks.

With my camera and tripod at the ready, I approached the giant web of moss-covered limbs cautiously, as if they would lunge and drag me in if I wandered too close – perhaps to feed me to the Wisht

Hounds. I imagined them silently waiting to pounce, having only spared me last night because they preferred a hearty breakfast to a late supper.

Thanks for sticking around, Gollum...

Positioning my tripod on the uneven, spongy ground between the rocks would be a challenge. This piece of kit was essential here, though; not enough light filtered through the tree canopy to enable a fast shutter speed, and using flash would spoil the evenly-distributed, natural light. After a few disappointments, I managed to capture a satisfactory image.

I visited two more locations at the edge of the trees. At the last I was presented with my favourite image of Wistman's Wood, courtesy of a tree that appeared to pose for me. Or perhaps 'remains of a tree' would be a more accurate description.

Even smaller than its neighbours, it stemmed from a narrow trunk, sprouting two branches for arms, complete with elbows but missing hands. The knee of his only leg was bent slightly, as if he were about to launch into a Broadway number (although I wouldn't describe this tree-man as disabled; his confident stance gave the impression he'd been destined to be a monoped). One arm waved at me, the other almost touched the ground. Although possessing no foliage, he was dressed from head to toe in the same coat of green moss as everything else in this wood. A far cry from how I'd previously judged this plant, it appeared to be the lifeblood of my dancing tree, as he proudly took his place alongside the trunks of his forefathers.

After capturing my final shot of Wistman's Wood, I bid farewell to my friend and exited the trees. I didn't return to the path straight away, though. I'd exhausted my water supply and, having drunk just one litre since leaving the campsite, lethargy was starting to take hold of me, accompanied by a headache. I'd been slack throughout my hike when it came to drinking enough water. The orange tint of the urine I'd expelled, on average only once a day, was enough to tell me that. This was the first time I'd felt genuinely dehydrated, though, so couldn't put it off any longer; I would *have* to find a way down to the river.

At the far end of the wood I came upon a faint path that appeared to lead to the riverbank – only to find the route blocked by a stagnant pond, merely a stones' throw from the river. A few stumps of firm-looking grass poked out of the smelly, muddy water, two or three feet apart and leading to a tiny tributary. After removing my pack I leapt across four of them to arrive alongside the trickle of water. I dropped to my knees, then recoiled at the nauseating stench of fresh cowpats – courtesy of a few cows penned into an enclosure that included part of the pond, extending right up to the edge of Wistman's Wood.

As disgusting as the pond was, the water trickling into it from the tiny stream was clear and fast-flowing. I told myself it would do. After all, no Dartmoor spring water had made me ill so far. Come to think of it, nothing had. Although the moors had been lacking in bathing facilities, I'd routinely sanitised my hands before every meal. Humans are too obsessed with hygiene in the twenty-first century, anyway. This is partly why we are now frequently bombarded by news reports warning of drug-resistant infections, or viral pandemics in years to come. A bit of dirt or a dose of illness is good for us every once in a while; it gives our immune systems a kick up the ass.

I filled my bottle and popped in a trusty chlorine pill, then hopped back across the islands. Back on dry land, the cows glared at me as I perched on a grassy stump.

'Cheers, girls!' I said, a little pompously, as I raised my bottle to them. I almost took a sip…then remembered that I needed to let the pill work its magic first.

I crossed a stile built into a drystone wall, where a sign marked the boundary of Wistman's Wood Nature Reserve. I then followed the path as it descended gently along the valley. After about a mile I would reach the tiny village of Two Bridges, then head south-west along the B3212 to the much larger village of Princetown, grabbing some lunch before taking a path across Walkhampton Common, finishing up the day at a place called Foggintor Quarry.

The path led me to a small car park which doubled as a bus stop. To my left stood the cliff-face of a disused quarry, partially concealed behind a huge oak tree. Across the road stood the Two Bridges Hotel and Restaurant.

My plan had been to walk the short distance (roughly another mile) to Princetown along this road. However, after observing the sparse yet speedy traffic along the route, a study of the timetable at the bus stop revealed that I had time to catch the last of the two daily services.

The thought also occurred to me that I could stick around here a little longer and treat myself to lunch at the restaurant. For a second consecutive day, my stomach was bucking the trend and beginning to growl in the middle of the day. After faffing about on two previous occasions trying to get some pub grub inside me, here was an opportunity begging to be taken. No doubt I appeared a little unkempt…but I wasn't looking for a table at The Ritz. The few customers dining in the beer garden were dressed not hugely dissimilar to myself. Although granted, they probably smelled better.

After gazing dreamily at the pub for a few moments, I crossed the road and strolled along to one of the two bridges that had awarded this place its name.

Below me, to the left of the West Dart River, a massive, well-manicured lawn extended right up to the riverbank, forming part of the pub's beer garden, in which a couple of swans pecked at the grass. Behind the garden, another hump-backed bridge crossed the river downstream, allowing a narrow lane to serve as a back-entrance to the hotel. Beyond that bridge, in stark contrast to the smooth lawn before me, the wild heathland of the moor resumed.

More cars whizzed past, each accompanied by a gust of air turbulence. Finally convinced that walking to Princetown wasn't such a good idea, I headed back to the bus stop.

Minutes later my ride popped into view, so I hailed it down.

'You're better off waitin' 'ere – I'll be comin' back round in about twenty minutes,' the driver informed me in a matter-of-fact tone, after I'd climbed aboard to inform him of my destination. 'It'll cost ya another two quid if you get on now.'

Even as tight-fisted as I was, I had no objections to paying an extra two quid for a longer ride. In fact, an extra 20 minutes of sitting on a dry, cushioned seat sounded like a bargain at that price. Something, however, compelled me to heed his advice.

'Oh right. Okay, cheers,' I replied, vacantly, then I turned and stepped back down onto the car park.

Minutes after the bus pulled off I was wishing I'd taken that extra-long ride, as something skewered the clouds and rain began hammering down, forcing me to take shelter beneath the tree. But sure enough the bus soon re-appeared, approaching from the opposite direction before pulling over again. The driver beamed as I climbed aboard.

'You might be a bit damp, but you can treat yourself to a pint, now!' he declared, in a light-hearted tone of feigned wisdom, with a smile at the corner of his mouth.

'Yeah, cheers. I might just do that,' I chuckled. He informed me of the bargain fare that I'd stood in the rain for, to which I handed over a few coins, then I planted my pack and myself into a seat near the front of the bus.

My amusement at his joke was genuine – the words I responded with, less-so. Whilst it would have been glorious to feel the head of a nice ale tickling my moustache, and whilst I'd considered stopping off at the Two Bridges Restaurant, as the bus rattled off up the road I realised how self-conscious I'd become about my appearance. It was a feeling that had grown steadily since I'd glared into that mirror at the campsite. The passengers had paid only marginal attention to me as I'd boarded the bus, yet I imagined eyes boring into the back of my glowing red head. No doubt there would be a pub or two in Princetown – but in my mind, my entrance into any of them would be reminiscent of that classic scene from *An American Werewolf in*

London (one of my favourite movies), where the two ill-fated American backpackers walk into a bustling Yorkshire pub (*The Slaughtered Lamb*) in the middle of nowhere, and the place falls deathly silent.

I couldn't be doing with that. Stick to the plan, I told myself. At least until after you've found another bush next to a stream – where you can wash your armpits and testicles.

Almost immediately after the bus had set off, the rain ceased and the clouds fizzled away. Finally the sun was re-born, to its brightest afternoon since my 'swim' two days before. Dazzling flashes of sunlight bounced off the wet tarmac, followed by plumes of steam.

Then, having barely gotten comfy in my seat, the rolling moorland dissolved into a grey, urban collage, and the bus pulled over. All the other passengers alighted, but I was under the impression there was another stop in the centre of the village – so I stayed put as the bus pulled away and weaved through the streets of Princetown.

This large village was by far the most urbanised area I'd seen since leaving Okehampton, and at 435 metres above sea level, Princetown carries the distinction of being the highest settlement across Dartmoor National Park. Its infrastructure measured less than a square kilometre on the map, with the only prominent feature being a distinctive, neat circle drawn at the north end of the village: Dartmoor Prison.

Initially built as a military prison in 1809, the facility closed during peacetime, re-opening to house civilian offenders in 1851. It would go on to incarcerate some of the UK's worst offenders of the twentieth century. The prison's remote location ensured that whichever direction they gambled on, any escapees would face a gruelling trek across Dartmoor's unforgiving heathland and peat bogs – usually resulting in a swift apprehension.

Whilst peat bogs and mud may not sound particularly dangerous, there is plenty of evidence of the perils this terrain can inflict on the unsuspecting walker (or prison escapee), including accounts of walkers requiring rescue from the mud by the emergency services. One of the most treacherous areas of Dartmoor, avoided by even the most accomplished hikers, is Fox Tor Mires: a boggy region south of Princetown, which has inspired tales of hauntings by the ghosts of prisoners who'd perished after succumbing to the quagmire.

Today, having been downgraded to a Category-C prison, HMP Dartmoor houses mostly non-violent offenders. In recent years the site has hosted an annual 'Prison-Break' event, in which members of the public attempt to escape and evade capture, with the entry fees raising money for worthy causes. In 2011, TV presenter James May took part in a mock escape attempt as part of his programme, *James May's Man Lab*. In a few years' time the prison will be fully consigned to history, as the UK government has confirmed its intention to close the facility for good.

Whilst somewhat intriguing, the prison couldn't tempt me to delay my return to the moorland. The limited view of its exterior from the bus was enough to satisfy my curiosity.

My return to the moor almost was delayed, however, thanks to my misreading of the bus timetable; the bus stopped only once in Princetown. My suspicion was aroused as the empty bus shifted up a gear and began to pick up speed, replacing my urban view from the window with that of the moorland. My puzzled face met the driver's eyes through the rear-view mirror.

'Where are you gettin' off, mate?' he asked.

'Sorry...I thought you made another stop in the village...' Shuffling down the aisle, I felt like a prize-plonker as the bus pulled over. The driver gave a forgiving laugh.

'Noooo...next stop is Dousland, about fifteen minutes away,' he advised, playfully.

He wished me well as I thanked him, then I stepped down onto the grass verge at the roadside. After watching the bus drive away, I walked back into the centre of the village. Still keen to avoid the dreaded couscous whenever possible, I nipped into a shop and treated myself to a sandwich, a bar of chocolate, and a fizzy drink, taking care not to send any stock flying from the shelves with my cumbersome backpack.

I sat and ate on the village green. Assorted hikers, cyclists and canoeists intermittently pulled over at the nearby coach park, seemingly only to use the public toilets. I watched in amusement as strangers traded small change to unlock the toilet door; there was a small charge to use the facilities. Those rays of sunshine that had glinted on the road had been short-lived, and the air was still muggy. A few light rumbles of thunder reverberated overhead, and at one point I felt a sprinkling of rain.

Once I'd finished my lunch I needed to visit the toilet myself, so I rummaged through my pockets for some change. It was just as well that I only needed to use the urinal; I would have barely squeezed into the cubicle with my pack in tow.

I studied my reflection in the mirror. It had changed little since the last time I'd done so. I splashed some water over my face. Then, map in hand, I set off for the path that would lead me to Foggintor Quarry.

I left the road not far from where I'd stepped off the bus. Hosting numerous fellow walkers, canines, cyclists and joggers, this path was by far the busiest route I'd been on since crossing Whitchurch Common. At first I was surprised at the popularity of Walkhampton Common, then I remembered that this was a Saturday afternoon. The moor was hosting both holidaymakers and locals – although no-one in sight carried anything even close to the size of my pack.

As I proceeded across Walkhampton Common, an assortment of huge storm clouds approached from the western horizon. Their fluffy tops contrasted starkly with the sagging, inky-blue bulges of their underbellies.

After a while I reached a point where the path forded a stream (although the current was virtually non-existent, to the point where the ford resembled a huge puddle). Further ahead, the same stream had carved through a small hill, forming a mini canyon in the process. Here, a strip of marshy ground replaced the stream, heading through the canyon into a huge, rocky enclosure.

Ditching the path, I picked my way up the hill, noting the significantly decreased human population around me and the increased one of sheep. Near the top I gazed over the edge of the steep bank down to the stream, then observed the cliff-encircled hideaway beyond.

This *had* to be Foggintor Quarry; my intended camping location.

Quarrying began at this site in the 1820s. In the mid-nineteenth century much of its rock was shipped to London to form Nelson's Column – amongst other noted landmarks of the capital. At times, over 300 men worked at Foggintor, but in 1906 the quarry was abandoned in favour of an alternative site at nearby Swelltor. Since being decommissioned, the Foggintor site has been reclaimed by nature and is now regularly cited as a top Dartmoor attraction. It is also a popular location for wild swimming – although I had yet to locate any substantial water feature within it. Although not situated within any military range, Foggintor is another site often used as a training ground by the British Forces.

Just as I was about to head higher still, the sound of nearby voices stopped me in my tracks. Some were discussing their present whereabouts; others were more concerned with whether the ground would be too rocky to pitch on, or discussing 'rope techniques'. My heart sank as I realised I was not going to have the quarry to myself. This was selfish, I know, but I'd become accustomed to having my own private campsite every night.

A faint rumble of thunder announced itself to the west. I watched from my vantage point as four youths appeared at the base of the cliff below me. Upon sighting not only their tents, but also ropes and various other equipment, my last remaining shred of doubt as to their intentions slipped away over the rock face. Their voices failed to fall in decibels as they moved deeper into the quarry, with three more of them emerging from the enclosed entrance to the canyon. The second bunch looked a few years older – but followed their cohorts with the same level of indiscretion.

In my experience, and at the risk of sounding like a grumpy old man, camping within earshot of a gang of youths usually meant only one thing: a sleepless night. The first time I'd suffered this issue was up in Scotland many years ago, when a crowd of rowdy teenagers pitched up at the campsite a few days after my arrival. Around midnight, as I lay in my tent, unable to sleep thanks to their partying, I heard the gruff voice of a much older, angrier Scot. After a lot of shouting the youths were chucked off the site right there and then. On another occasion, camping in Northumberland, a couple of Geordie lads had returned to their tent after last orders, absolutely plastered. Dressed in her nightie, the sweet old lady who ran the site came out to ask them to be quiet, but they still rambled on at the tops of their voices after she'd gone back indoors. Karma prevailed though, when one of them announced that he'd pissed himself inside his sleeping bag. I poked my head outside at dawn to find they'd made a discreet, early exit.

Would tonight provide another such incident?

Then, seeming to hear my thoughts, one of the younger members of the troupe turned to face me.

'Excuse me,' he bellowed. 'Is this Foggintor Quarry?'

I shouted back that it was. Not rudely, but without wishing to engage in conversation. The lad who'd posed the question showed no interest in chatting either; he'd turned back round almost before I'd finished answering him.

I was being judgemental. I couldn't help it. But whilst I'd had bad experiences with groups of young campers before, what I'd failed to consider here was that all those incidents had occurred on campsites. That is the main reason why so many campsites refuse to accept large groups of young adults (see – I'm not the only one stereotyping...). It's probably also one of the reasons why wild camping is still illegal across almost all of England and Wales; there is an inherent assumption that should the law ever be relaxed, hordes of unsavoury characters would descend upon the countryside, leaving untold destruction in their wake after pulling up their tent pegs. Sadly, those beer cans I'd found near Meldon Reservoir gave weight to that assumption. But one could also argue that should more of the countryside be made available to campers, we would develop a greater respect for it. But at what cost? What cost until we reached such a time when people could be trusted with nature? And is it a naïve assumption that those who would prefer to camp wild would automatically have a greater respect for the countryside than those who preferred the campsites? Either way, my neighbours at least deserved the benefit of the doubt, so rather than lord over them in self-righteousness, I left them to it, seeking out my own pitch as those storm-bearing clouds drifted closer.

I decided against camping on the highest part of the cliff. Not just to avoid the wind, but to maintain a little privacy. I therefore selected one of the flat grassy ledges lower down.

The tent was still damp after packing it away in the rain that morning (again), so after erecting the inner layer I spread the flysheet out to dry, hoping the next downpour would hold off a little longer. In the meantime I headed back up the hill, in search of a supreme view of Walkhampton Common beneath those dramatic clouds.

I casually looked out over the quarry. The youngsters had now pitched two tents. Two of them were finishing off a third and a few others were building a fire nearby. Would they be using a flint and steel like I'd attempted on my first day? If so, would they be rewarded with any greater measure of success...?

Of far greater interest, though, was the vista sprawling across the landscape to the west of the quarry. On the left, a second rock formation named Black Tor capped a gentle peak. Beyond, a few miles away, a coniferous woodland enclosed a grey sliver of Burrator Reservoir, pushing back against the clouds. In the centre of the scene, but nearly a kilometre away and spread a few hundred metres apart, three distinct rock formations topped Walkhampton Common. To this day I am only sure of the identity of one of them: Kings Tor – the one furthest right of the trio. To the north-west, the common stepped back, revealing an expanse of hills beyond, dominated by what I suspected was Great Staple Tor. Beneath them sat a solitary white house, close to which the Merrivale Quarry had gouged out a huge grey chunk from the hillside. Was that the Merrivale Inn – the pub I'd sought out during my first pub-hunt? To the north – the extreme right of my view – the moors stretched on, uninterrupted, all the way to Okehampton, although the peaks of Great Mis Tor and Black Dunghill, a few miles away, curtailed the view in that direction.

Before all of this, perched upon a small grassy ledge alongside Foggintor Quarry, sat the naked inner layer of my tiny tent, waiting patiently for me to come back down and dress it.

But I wasn't finished up here, yet; I'd brought my camera gear with me, and once I was done shooting stills I took out my camcorder. I slowly panned across the vista, taking in the rear of the quarry, too, whilst its occupants shot bullets of laughter and chatter into the quiet evening air.

'Sarah – do you realise you're being watched?' one of the boys called out. A girl amongst the group paused from her horsing around, glancing up in my direction. Although her friend's words had been spoken in a jovial tone, for a moment I worried that my neighbours might assume I was a pervert. My concern wasn't sufficient to deter me from documenting my location, though. Neither did 'Sarah' or her friends follow up on that comment. In fact, their decibel-level decreased immediately, perhaps aware for the first time since their arrival that others were trying to enjoy the quarry, too.

With my filming completed, I sat and watched the shadows of clouds drift across the common. This must have sent me into something of a meditative state, as I failed to notice not only the strengthening wind but also the arrival of the storm clouds overhead. A thunderclap boldly announced itself and splats of rain began to hit my arms. I snapped to attention and raced back to my pitch.

The sky flashed. Then it roared.

The rain gathered pace and a few high-pitched squeals left the quarry. Squeals that I shared internally but managed to contain as I threw the flysheet over the tent. For some reason the same excitement had eluded me during the storms of the previous evening. Perhaps I was still adjusting to the physicality of being back on the moor. Or was I pre-occupied with the concern of being camped illegally, or the possibility of being devoured by the Wisht Hounds...? Whatever the reason, it was unlike me to have turned my back on a storm. I had always wanted to capture a dramatic lightning-shot. Whilst I'd enjoyed a modicum of success in this field of photography, I was yet to achieve something fully satisfying.

Much closer to the south, the second lightning bolt struck. The thunder followed almost immediately; a high-pitched crackle that tumbled to an impatient snarl, like a descending scale from the overture of a tragic opera.

There was no time to peg the flysheet down. I dragged my pack inside then set up my camera.

Photographing an electrical storm is one of the greatest challenges to a landscape photographer – for the obvious reason that one never knows exactly when or where the lightning will strike. For a successful shot the camera has to be mounted on a tripod, then you frame your shot, focus to infinity, set a long exposure time – and trust to luck that the lightning will strike somewhere in the frame whilst the shutter is open. The main challenge is the issue of over-exposure due to the shutter being open for so long. To combat this, a filter is used to block out most of the light, while still allowing the bright flashes of lightning through as the rest of the image gradually imprints on the sensor. The key to success is in balancing the correct shutter speed against the amount of light you allow through the filter.

My previous thunderstorm photos had been captured at night – removing the issue of over-exposure. However, replacing that element of the challenge *here* was the fact that I didn't possess a filter for my wide-angle lens. I would therefore be forced to use my 35mm lens and filter, but as its field of view is much smaller, the odds of a lightning bolt striking somewhere within the frame of my shot would be considerably reduced. So, in short, to achieve my desired shot I would be relying on luck even more than usual.

With my camera fixed to the tripod, I framed a composition, focussed on the clouds, then rotated the filter into position. I took a few test shots, tweaking the settings. As I did so the clouds spat out another couple of lightning bolts, each roaring with mocking laughter.

Eventually satisfied with the settings, I began firing off a sequence of shots, each with an exposure time of eight seconds. As I sheltered just inside the tent, my eyes raced between the violent symphony raging across the sky, and the largely-vacuous grey images on the camera's rear display. A few bolts looked like they may have struck within the frame, but I knew better than to raise my expectations.

No more than ten minutes passed between the first and final flashes. Then the dark clouds passed and the rain eased off.

As the thunderstorm bid farewell, I reviewed my efforts. They were more or less as I'd expected. A few shots featured patches of illuminated clouds, courtesy of some achingly-close strikes, but only one image contained any actual electricity: just the tip of a bolt at the edge of the frame.

As it had done so on many an occasion, my enduring pessimism came to the rescue of my mood.

Later on I ventured back up to the edge of the quarry, where my neighbours had suspended ropes from the cliff-tops above their camp. I watched as two of them began descending the rock-face. Although I've always been an outdoors enthusiast, I can't say this pursuit has ever carried much appeal to me. I wouldn't have the dexterity for it – or the head for heights. But to great applause and cheers from their friends, the youngsters reached the bottom of the cliff with ease. For a second I contemplated joining in with the celebration, but considering how they'd already suspected me of perving at them, I thought better of it. As another pair prepared to emulate their friends' success, I headed back down the hill.

More fierce-looking clouds drifted overhead throughout the evening, but despite a few rumbles the rain held off. The only other sounds came courtesy of an occasional bleating sheep and more faint cheering from my neighbours.

After dinner I teased another couple of shots from the landscape, before the golden-hour clouds melted away and the sun disappeared behind Kings Tor. In the waning light, the expectant mist nestled at the tips of the rocks, in a pale, yellow-grey shroud of familiarity that floated from the sky like a silken scarf.

Eventually the cheers ceased; my neighbours were retiring for the evening. I wondered where they might be heading tomorrow, and about what kind of conversations they might be having as they huddled around their campfire. Over the past ten days I'd spoken to no more than a dozen people, in conversations that probably averaged about ten seconds each. By contrast, two weeks previously I was having my ears chewed off all day long by displeased customers in my call-centre job. The sudden absence from my life of any human interaction hadn't really bothered me – until now.

Suddenly I wished for someone to share the evening with. To share this amazing view; the tranquillity; the thrill of the thunderstorm and the complexities of photographing it. But even with company, I would have been content just to sit and gaze over the landscape in a comfortable silence.

Because a comfortable silence is also a beautiful thing to share. A moment of peace without awkwardness. Then I reminded myself that this was my hike and mine alone. I was doing what I wanted, when I wanted, and at my own pace.

Most of my camping trips before and since this one have been solitary experiences, as I enjoy, perhaps selfishly, not having to burden myself with anyone else's wishes or concerns along the way. Less selfishly, though, I also hate slowing others down. Most of my friends have always been in better shape than myself, and should they find themselves in my company on any hillwalking expedition, they would be forced to either leave me trailing behind, or take frequent breaks so I could catch up.

Such was the case when I climbed Snowdon a few years back. We'd taken the tourist-friendly Llanberis Path – but even so, by the time I'd reached the summit my friends had all been sat around the cairn, in a biting wind, for quite a while.

At least on Dartmoor my struggles had remained private.

As I reflected on my time here, that sense of loneliness faded with the landscape, as the evening mist thickened before adopting a subtle, rosé-tinted hue.

Once the tors had fully succumbed to the haze, I retired for the evening, looking forward to another day of unashamed selfishness tomorrow.

Chapter Eight: Water and Technology

Foggintor Quarry to Yennadon Down

Upon waking alongside Foggintor Quarry, I was struck by the unusual silence of the morning. I'd become accustomed to being woken by the gentle sounds of birdsong, wind, or a trickling stream. Lying in my tent in the middle of the countryside – as opposed to being on a campsite, probably not far from a road, house, railway line or other campers – amplified those sparse sounds, accentuating the silence that engulfed me from outside the radius of a few metres beyond my tent. A bird tweeting, for example, became a comforting siren. But right there and then, nothing disturbed this hushed start to the day, other than the occasional rustle of the flysheet as a gentle breeze drifted over the quarry.

I began to contemplate what photos I might capture in the day ahead. Pony pictures aside, I was fairly satisfied with what I'd snapped so far. There'd been one or two missed opportunities, for sure, but I'd also decided early on that I would not allow my photography to become forced, and more importantly, that this hike demanded certain moments should remain for my eyes only.

Whilst none of Dartmoor's climatic conditions had yet afforded me a classic postcard view, I had learned to appreciate this as part of the distinctive charm of the region. I reflected on my time camping by the reservoir, on how I'd longed for that cliché shot of colourful dawn clouds over the water. I'm not saying that would have been a scene unworthy of capturing; if that shot would have been on offer I would have taken it. But ultimately I wanted my Dartmoor photography to capture images that couldn't be captured anywhere else. Such a philosophy demanded that I embraced not just the unique landscape, but also its niche climate. So, whilst it was fair to say that not every photography session had been a successful one – my definition of success was broadening. And there were four days to go, yet...

I pulled on my boots and stepped outside.

A thick fog had descended over the common, smothering all but the craggy hillside that partially enclosed the patch of grass outside my tent. The epic vista of tors and hills had been swallowed up by a vast, white void. Barely discernible, a few sheep shuffled along the path that passed the quarry.

Beyond, there was nothing.

I put on my fleece and headed up to the cliff-edge with my camera and wide-angle lens. A mini-Steadicam system would have been handy at this point, too, of the kind I'd researched online as I'd become more and more seduced by my hobby. That type of gear was beyond my budget, though. Not to mention the fact that I had barely enough room in pack as it was. Hand-held video would have to do.

I passed along the edge of the cliff, peering into the depths of the quarry, tracing the path those youths had followed as far as possible before it disappeared into the white shroud. Unlike the glowing billows that had swept over Whitchurch Common, the fog drifted around me in the subtlest variations of density. As I headed further around the cliff, nearer to where my neighbours had camped, a dark blob crept out of the fog; the pond.

Had camped; there was no trace that anyone had ever been there. At what hour had they gotten up to have departed already? I then realised the error in my judgement of those youngsters. They hadn't made a peep since dusk. In fact, I'd slept better than I had during any other night so far.

I stopped filming and reviewed the clip. To my amazement, my camera displayed a recording time of 08:47. I couldn't believe I'd slept in so late. At first I was annoyed with myself...but fog this thick would have most likely been lingering since well before dawn, so I doubted that I'd missed out on any decent photo opportunities.

The fog carried a light drizzle, although had it not been for the tiny specks of rain on the camera, I would never have noticed. Pausing frequently to wipe the lens with toilet paper, I continued along the cliff-edge, reaching the point from where the kids had abseiled down the rock-face. I leaned over and peered down the crack that marked their route. A few seconds of gazing down at the hazy, rocky ground below was enough to elevate my admiration for them – as well as induce a slight sense of vertigo.

After exploring a little more of the cliff-top, I made for the path and headed towards the remnants of the quarry buildings a short distance away. The crunch of my boots on the gritty track seemed intrusively loud; eerie, even, amidst the otherwise-silent, vacuous landscape. Consequently, I approached the ruined buildings with the poise of a trespasser.

By now the fog had thinned a little, revealing a few mini-quarries to the left of the path, preceding the buildings. These dug-outs had been shored up here and there by stone walls which, although crumbling in places, chopped into the moorland like huge steps, over a metre high and covered with moss and lichen. Built into one of the walls was the entrance to a sunken corridor, leading into what had once been an underground chamber of some sort. Above it stood another lichen-encrusted wall, maybe a dozen metres long and half that at its highest point, having been chopped diagonally where the rest of the wall had fallen away. To my disappointment I would not be entering the chamber; a closer inspection revealed that the corridor had been deliberately sealed by rocks long ago.

The rest of the buildings, whilst no less intriguing, were even less substantial than those I'd come across on my way to Wistman's Wood, and had clearly proved no match for Dartmoor's cruel winters (or her cruel summers, one could argue) once abandoned to the elements. Whilst yet to experience the full spectrum of this microclimate, I was under no illusion that I would escape its full force during my remaining time here. I had certainly experienced some of its quirks; here I was, in the middle of June, yet strolling amidst a dense fog that was lingering on well past dawn. The only other place in which I'd found myself embroiled in a summer fog was at the summit of Ben Nevis, back in my younger (and much fitter) days.

Back at the tent I looked forward to my usual bowl of porridge, having eaten only a few shortbread biscuits – not even with my limp interpretation of tea – the previous morning. My water bottle was almost empty, though, so I headed down to where the boggy stream left the quarry and bore some semblance of flowing water, near the massive puddle I'd dodged on my way here.

Selecting a relatively clear spot, I scraped out a little trench, fashioning a tiny dam of pebbles at one end which would serve as a crude filter. After filling my bottle I studied the contents closely. Amongst the particles suspended in the water was a miniscule insect of some kind – identifiable only by the presence of a few legs. I discarded that attempt, but another half a dozen fillings yielded similar results. Eventually realising I was never going to get a crystal-clear serving, I settled for a bottleful that at least appeared to be free of bugs, then popped in a chlorine pill and strolled back to the tent.

By lunchtime the fog was still lingering, but with visibility up to about half a kilometre, I finally said goodbye to Foggintor Quarry and proceeded further across Walkhampton Common, heading south-west towards a place called Yennadon Down. According to my research, this place offered fabulous views over nearby Burrator Reservoir. My route first backtracked some way along the path that had brought me here, then led me onto a track that would pass another rock formation – Ingra Tor.

With the fog lifting not long after I set off, Walkhampton Common turned out to be perhaps the prettiest and lushest stretch of moorland I'd crossed so far. More than just a heathland, ferns, shrubs and blossom-draped hawthorn trees were abound. To the teams of ponies I passed, this was surely the Garden of Eden. As always, this charming region of the moor also lay before a fabulous backdrop of hills – capped by the obligatory tor here and there.

As morning gave way to afternoon, the overcast sky gave way to pillows of fluffy clouds, occasionally releasing light showers through the sporadic sunshine. But with the humidity of the past couple of days notably absent, I was now enjoying – finally – the perfect weather for hiking.

Less absent was the presence of fellow walkers. At one point I was stopped by a friendly, elderly couple, who enquired if I was walking the West Devon Way (although I was a few miles east of that trail). They seemed unsurprised and not particularly impressed when I summarised my route to them, but they clearly shared my love of the outdoors and wished me well.

I stood at the end of a bridge over a small gulley. Standing guard before me, fixed to the top of a fence post, was a huge, snarling, yellowing skull. I deduced that it was most likely the remains of a cow (I also found the idea of it being that of a pony less palatable).

The skull bore two rows of flat teeth, set in a maniacal grin stretching halfway around its head. Reminding me of the braces I'd worn on my own teeth as a child, these jaws had been secured with wires, aided by a length of old, gnarled rope. The eye sockets were spread wide apart, whilst a narrow ridge swelled up along the snout, forming a blunt spike somewhere close to where, in the beast's previous life, a pair of nostrils might have snorted a warning at me to find an alternative route across the gulley. A tattered piece of cloth clung to the back of the skull.

Although skulls have always intrigued me with their dark-comedic value, this I found a little macabre; not the kind of thing a young child might want to come across whilst wandering along the path. It was certainly nothing like the remains of other animal heads I'd seen. I am no skull connoisseur – but I've seen a few. The most memorable of which crossed my path during the years I stacked supermarket shelves for a living...

Our in-store butcher had somehow ended up with a pig's head from one of his suppliers. After failing to offload the thing to his motley crew of customers, he gifted it to me. How generous, you may be thinking. Perhaps. But he'd also staved off boredom earlier in the day by throwing its gouged-out eyeballs at me in the stockroom. So in my book, he owed me.

Although not entirely sure what purpose it would serve, and with the thing sufficiently wrapped in bin liners, I carried the head home at the end of my shift. Maybe I'd turn it into some kind of ornament...a paperweight, perhaps? Knowing my mum would go barmy and chuck it straight in the dustbin if she clapped eyes on it, I kept the thing wrapped up and hidden behind our garden shed until I could get to work on it.

A few days later I had the house to myself. So, equipped with the same knife with which my mum had carved up our Sunday roast just hours before, I set to work. Unfurling the plastic bags, I recoiled at the putrid stench that escaped from within – a weird blend of gone-off meat and sawdust, reminding me of the time when, as a kid, I discovered my mangy pet hamster dead in his cage.

Holding my breath, I began to hack away at the flesh and gristle, managing to remove the ears and some of the snout. Regardless of my butchery skills, though, I could tolerate that stench only so long before admitting defeat. Instead, I decided to take the head out somewhere and bury it, under the assumption that after a few weeks most of the flesh would have rotted away. I'd then dig it up, take it back home and boil the thing up to finish the job. Assuming I could find a pot big enough, of course... After wiping blood and slivers of flesh from my mum's knife, I wrapped up the skull and carried it down to the canal towpath after dark, then laid it to rest in a shallow grave behind some bushes.

When I returned a few weeks later it was gone. Not a trace of the thing remained. I still frequently walk along that stretch of the canal, and to this day, as I pass by those bushes, I often wonder about the fate of my pig's head.

Anyway, that was the first and last time I messed about with animal heads – although I could still appreciate an interesting skull whenever one crossed my path. This one had grown on me after the resurfacing of that memory, so as those bare bovine teeth grinned back at me, I couldn't help reciprocating. I've been told on a few occasions that my teeth are my finest physical feature – but there was no way my gnashers could compete with *that* smile.

Of course, I had to capture the skull on camera. I've always found something inexplicably alluring in photographing dead things. And not just skulls; foxes, mice, pigeons, swans. All have served as my muse through their untimely demise. My favourite of the past few years, though, was probably a decomposing frog that I once shared a park bench with whilst eating lunch. In comparison to what I did for a living at the time, that lunch-date provided the highlight of my day. But despite my fascination with skulls I don't think I'm a psychopath. I have no plans to resort to grave robbing or homicide, or poisoning my neighbour's smelly gerbils, to satisfy my urges.

An hour or two later my route curled around a steep hill capped by Ingra Tor. Soon after I sighted a few parked vehicles in the mid-distance, and within half an hour I was standing at the edge of a car park beside the B3212, enjoying a cool treat courtesy of an ice cream van.

I then left Walkhampton Common for a path on the other side of the road, leading me to a coniferous woodland. Soon the road was out of sight again, and on approaching the trees I spotted a young couple a short distance in front, heading in the same direction as myself. The guy, in particular, appeared to be fixated with his mobile phone. As I drew closer, I realised they were using it for navigation.

This was the first time I'd seen a walker ditching a paper map in favour of this modern alternative. Rather them than me. Maybe I'm a little old-fashioned. No – I definitely am – and probably more than a little. But justifiably so, I think. We rely on technology far too much in modern life. One day it will be the end of us. What would happen, I wonder, if every computer in the world suddenly stopped working? And am I the only one who's seen *The Terminator*? I'm not just talking about machines becoming self-aware and rising up against us, either. The decline of our species has already begun. Already being eroded away are our social skills, self-confidence and our willingness to learn and develop at a natural pace. It all began a long time ago under the subliminal guise of video games. Now we demand instant, interactive gratification – unable to invest ourselves in subtler media, or recreational pursuits that require us to develop our skills over time.

Then along came social media – and now we must be in constant contact with everyone, all the time. Because we think *this* is socialising. We no longer want to learn how to do anything for ourselves. Not even how to boil an egg or slice an onion. Take a guess at how many videos cover such 'tasks' on Youtube. I don't know the number – but trust me, it's a lot. I must confess that learning how to boil an egg or slice an onion, all by myself, has never given me any real sense of achievement. But learning certain other skills has. My photography is a case in point – in which I continue to learn. And the way I've learnt is, essentially, by making mistakes. But now we refuse to allow ourselves to make mistakes. Mistakes are bad. Mistakes are a sign of failure. We expect instant success in everything we do, seeking tangible validation from our peers in the form of 'likes'. If we fail to earn that validation, we judge ourselves negatively.

Social media has also impacted our ability to hold rational discussion. The subtleties of face-to-face (or even just voice-to-voice) communication can never be replicated online. As a result, comments quickly get misinterpreted or taken out of context.

Arguments become polarised. People demand that others be silenced, or even sacked from their job, simply for not agreeing with them. We call this phenomenon 'cancel culture' – yes, we even have a name for it.

And now, fuelled by social media, we have the rise of an entire sub-culture that not only wants to cancel those who disagree with them, but seeks to find offence or danger or social stigma in virtually anything. Such people believe we should ban applause and replace it with 'jazz hands' – on the grounds that, for a miniscule minority of people, the sound of applause may trigger an anxiety attack. In schools, we no longer differentiate between winning and losing. Because losing is bad for our mental health. So now they hand out 'participation prizes' instead of medals. Well guess what, folks: from the cradle to the grave, life is tough. Whether we like it or not, we will face competition and disappointment until the day we die. So how does wrapping kids up in cotton wool prepare them for life as an adult? All it does is make them even more vulnerable to mental health issues when they are finally immersed into the grown-up world. And all this is before we even delve into the subject of online bullying.

I have my own experience of mental health issues. I was prescribed medication to help me deal with it – but ultimately I had to help myself. And more importantly, my struggles with my mental health had nothing to do with technology or social media. Or the petrifying sound of applause.

The kids we are raising amongst this culture will one day be responsible for healing the sick; passing our laws; deciding whether or not we go to war. It doesn't bear thinking about.

Of course, the evil smartphone has played a key role in our downfall as a species. Unable to drag their eyes away from their phones, people don't even look where they're going anymore when they walk down the street. I mentioned about healing the sick – well doctors have reported that some medical students lack the dexterity in their fingers to master basic surgical skills. Why? Because they spent too much of their childhood screen-swiping, instead of building go-karts, or lego-sets, or dens in the woods. If you don't believe me, look it up. I've even seen young men with their phone in their hand whilst standing at a urinal. Not that I like to spend my free time watching men in public toilets, I might add…

Yes – I own a smartphone, too. But we are all slaves to technology up to a point; my good old Nokia 3210 was never going to last forever. My smartphone is ancient. It's the only one I've ever owned, and – ironically – the only 'smart' thing that still works on it is the sat-nav. I have so far resisted pressure from my peers to upgrade. The expiry date on the battery reads March 2012. I guess that might offer a crumb of comfort to some indigenous Argentinian tribesman, whose home is about to be bulldozed to make way for another lithium mine…

I'll also admit to using certain social media (I'm not a *total* dinosaur). In moderation, it can be a good thing – but I would never become addicted to it to the point where my sense of self-worth depends on how many 'likes' I get. When it comes to the degradation of my self-worth, I have far more culpable targets at which to spew my bile.

Just as strange as our obsession with smartphones, though, is the contradictory nature of our relationship with technology in general. For example, how often have you seen people arrive at a pedestrian crossing, see that the 'wait' sign is illuminated, indicating that the button has already been pressed, for them to then hammer away at the button anyway? Trust me, I see it a lot. We refuse to trust this basic technology that has been in use for nearly 100 years – but we will happily trust our lives to our phones. Now people are ditching maps in favour of phones, too. Where will it all end…?

Anyway, whether it be a smartphone map or a paper map, sighting this pair was the first time I'd seen anyone using a navigational tool of any kind since I'd arrived on Dartmoor. Then again, there had been only two areas on the moor where I'd experienced anything even close to what I could describe as pedestrian traffic: the commons of Whitchurch and Walkhampton. Was it simply the case that everyone else had a better sense of direction than me? Or had I been the only one around who was attempting a hike of any scale that necessitated a map? As the last lick of that ice cream dissolved in my mouth, I told myself it was the latter. Though I wasn't entirely convinced.

After a few minutes of deliberating, the couple headed east away from the forest and were soon out of sight. Heading in the opposite direction, I entered a corridor of towering conifers. The sweet, earthy scent of damp pine needles wafted through the air as I consulted my good old-fashioned paper map once more. Then I headed south through the woods towards Burrator Reservoir.

Soon the path met and ran alongside the Devonport Leat. This man-made stream once ran all the way to its namesake naval dockyards near Plymouth – a distance of 27 miles from its source: the weir I'd spotted on the West Dart River near Wistman's Wood. In post-industrialised Devon, however, the redundant leat terminated just a couple of miles away at the reservoir. The trickle of the water underscored a pleasant stroll through the evergreens as I followed its retaining wall, which carried the water waist-high alongside me.

A short while later I reached a small clearing, revealing the huge rocky rubble of Sheeps Tor at the tip of a broad hill on the other side of the reservoir, although the reservoir itself still lay somewhere below the treeline.

Deciding to take another break, I sat on the wall of the leat as the clouds alternately parted and converged, allowing sunlight to intermittently highlight the pale, gravelly bed beneath the water. It also illuminated shoals of tiny fish, darting through the current close to the surface. For a moment I was struck by the notion of trying to grab a few, on the grounds that they might make an interesting side dish to my portion of rice that evening. On the other hand, I'd never been massively keen on sushi, and eating those things would most likely only serve to get my bowels moving again.

Emerging from the woods a little later, I turned around to survey the leviathan of a hill that I'd caught glimpses of here and there, towering high above the treetops as I'd pushed on. Now, in all its glory, it appeared so steep that I would have struggled to get up there even without my pack. The map suggested the rocky outcrop at the top was Leather Tor. The view from up there would no doubt be spectacular – but I was saving myself for what awaited me at Yennadon Down.

The path then led me onto a lane, where Burrator Reservoir, now perhaps only half a mile away, finally revealed itself – albeit modestly. I was now just a mile or so from the edge of Yennadon Down – and my next excruciating climb.

Once the hill had succeeded in aging me by about ten years, the gradient took pity on me and levelled off. That climb had been steeper, in parts, than anything else I'd hiked so far on Dartmoor. Like a steam train grinding to a halt, my gushing breaths slowly eased, whilst my heart pounded furiously against my chest. I turned round on my doddery legs, expecting to observe the reservoir re-emerging from behind the trees below me. It didn't. Nevertheless, the views from the top of Yennadon Down were something special.

To the east, the moor tumbled back into the woods. Beyond the trees, wisps of white clouds clung to the swathes of grey that penned in the hills, forests and rocky outcrops. These included my first sighting of Sharpitor, overlooking the valley to the left, and the ever-dominant Sheeps Tor to the right. Both of these features climbed to about a hundred metres higher than my current location, with clouds jostling at their peaks. Yet here, roughly a mile away from both, I appeared virtually level with them, whilst right beneath my feet, Yennadon Down somehow remained beyond reach of the clouds.

Between those two tors, and behind the huge bowl in which the reservoir lay nestled below the treeline, the moor stretched beyond the coniferous woodland and onward to the horizon. An almost perfectly-conical grey peak marked the centre of this sweeping view, which I determined was most likely Down Tor, about two miles away. A little closer, to the right of Sharpitor, the tip of Leather Tor poked above the trees – daring me to venture back and scale it.

To the north, the moor extended only a kilometre or so, terminating at a row of trees, beyond which a few horses grazed on smooth pasture. To the south lay the tiny hamlet of Meavy, identified by the tower of its church. A more prominent, semi-urban sprawl lay about a mile further, which had to be the village of Yelverton. Trees also lined the western edge of this moor, closing off the land from the outside world and thus preserving its sense of isolation – despite the presence of populated areas less than an hour's walk away.

Chiefly, though, it was Yennadon Down itself that maintained the wilderness quality of this place. Everywhere else I'd camped, various features would point to the location of my tent to within a few hundred metres. But for the first time, I now found myself on an almost ubiquitous landscape, covered by virtually nothing but grass and gorse, the latter scorched in places by recent burns.

The grass was well cropped – no doubt by ponies, a few of which had congregated nearby. Unlike the shades of brown or grey of those I'd seen in other areas, these ponies all wore an assortment of black and white coats. They remained largely indifferent to my presence as I turned my attention to finding a pitch.

Open space was plentiful, but despite the sense of isolation this place evoked, I still wanted to camp discreetly. I also needed some kind of marker. Eventually I found a spot enclosed by bushes, with the distinct presence of a small hawthorn tree nearby. This pitch would be identifiable from no more than fifty metres away if I headed downhill, but it was the best I was going to find.

Despite the threatening clouds that swept overhead throughout the evening, the rain held off, whilst the occasional trot of hooves passed close by as I prepared my dinner. Closer, in fact, than I'd heard them on any previous occasion. Struck by the notion that the aroma of my chicken-flavoured rice might have attracted the ponies,

I zipped up the tent flap.

They allowed me to dine in peace, however, and once my full belly had settled, I headed out to find my water source: either one of a couple of streams that, according to the map, trickled into the reservoir at the bottom of the hill.

On my return, I identified my marker tree with only one or two minor deviations along the way. Had I finally fine-tuned my sense of direction to the level required of me on Dartmoor? If so, congratulations were in order; it had only taken me ten days…

The clouds had thinned a little during this excursion, and as I strolled back up the hill a few rays of watery sunlight drifted across Yennadon Down. As my elevation increased, revealing my pitch-marking tree, something else was revealed: a large dark shape, lurking around my tent.

A pony.

Its wild mane stroked at the polyester. Its nose keenly investigated the bottom of the flysheet. Mostly black with a few grey and white patches, the pony ignored me at first. Then, from about a dozen metres away, the animal cocked its head towards me. The eyes of the encroaching equine met mine, glinting in the soft sunlight. Then, with a twang, my tent shuddered as a hoof challenged a guy-line. Then the pony was gone, having retreated through the bushes.

The encroaching equine…??? Ha Ha!!! Ponies have been living on Dartmoor for more than 3,000 years. If there was any encroaching going on, I was the guilty party.

Following the departure of my visitor, I inspected the tent for pony slobber, then went inside and stripped off my dirty rags. The following morning I would dig out the last of my clean clothing, which would have to last me until I reached Ivybridge – and a launderette – in three days' time.

In the last usable offerings of natural light, I studied the map – specifically the route I would be taking tomorrow: a seemingly straightforward hike south-east, taking in two old abandoned houses, at Ditsworthy Warren and Nun's Cross Farm. I would be camping somewhere near the latter. My hike would then conclude with a comfortable, two-day stretch through what presented themselves as two of the most barren areas of the entire national park: Stall Moor and Erme Plains.

A large number of grid squares covered these areas on the map (each of which represented a square kilometre), containing almost nothing but contour lines and grass symbols. But amongst them were two features that had attracted my attention whilst planning my route. The first was a mile-long row of ancient stones. The second was another tiny patch of ancient woodland known as Piles Copse. These would serve as my last points of interest before my mud-splattered boots would carry me into the welcoming arms of Ivybridge.

As usual, I wasn't challenging myself in regard to my daily distances; over those final two days I would probably cover no more than nine or ten miles. Key to completing my intended route was my navigational skill – not my endurance. Despite my increased confidence, though, this factor still played on my mind a little. Then again, I *was* carrying a map and compass, and with my freshly-sharpened sense of direction in my armoury as well, those final two days would surely present no major problems.

Chapter Nine: The Housing Inspector

Yennadon Down to Nun's Cross Farm

Something heavy hit the ground a few feet from my chest. I jerked upright and my head hit the roof – much sooner that it should have done. Something huge pressed against the tent, pulling the rear end to the ground. Something barely visible in the pre-dawn twilight. Whatever was out there shifted around for a second or two…then it was gone.

The tent bounced back into shape with a thump. I gave my semi-awakened brain a moment to digest the incident, then unzipped the flap and peered outside. I hadn't had time to fumble around for my glasses, but could still make out a huge, blurry shape disappearing into the pre-dawn mist. Logically, it could only have been the ass-end of a pony.

I zipped up the tent, lay back down and imagined how else this incident might have ended, elaborating on the pony-related fantasy I'd dreamed up on Whitchurch Common. Now it concluded with my face squashed beneath that huge rump, whilst the other end of the beast rummaged through what remained of my porridge oats. Nothing but a couple of thin sheets of polyester would separate my face from its smelly backside. Only when he was done devouring my breakfast supplies would he get up, to shoot me a huge, toothy grin – his face decorated with flaky white oats – before swaggering off into the morning mist.

The mirth began to swell inside me as I mulled over that thought...before erupting into hoots of laughter.

Eventually I calmed down, turning my attention to the potential photography session that lay ahead at dawn. Perhaps this extra-early alarm call would work in my favour.

Fog had shrouded Yennadon Down, sparing only the bushes immediately around my tent; their vibrant greens and yellows bleached to a pale grey.

I decided to try something different: an ethereal shot of a pony emerging from the fog. One had rudely interrupted me earlier, so it seemed only fair that he or one of his mates should now pose for the camera. By this point I'd secured a few pony photos, but it was a somewhat disappointing section of my portfolio. Taken under drab, overcast skies and whimpering reluctantly onto the camera sensor, none of those images captured the true essence of these animals. I still had that half-decent camcorder footage of them on Cudliptown Down, of course, but thanks to their toilet habits, that clip would be unusable in its entirety.

With my zoom lens at the ready, I set off, anticipating coming across the ponies at any moment. Wary of wandering too far from the tent once my marker tree had vanished from view, I glanced back frequently to take note of my route.

The ponies remained elusive. I could have taken a few shots of the foggy flora, but this seemed a stale option. I had enough images of fog-filled landscapes already. Not to mention dwindling battery power for my camera.

What had begun as an exciting pony-hunt began to seem futile. I was also reaching the limit of my memory capacity with regards to finding my way back. If I did lose my way, I would have to wait until the fog lifted before being able to get back to the tent.

Minutes later I abandoned the search. For the first time on Dartmoor, the fog had left me a little disheartened.

That was my first disappointment of the day. Later, whilst disassembling the tent, came the second: on removing one of the two groundsheet hooks from the pole, I spotted a crack running a couple of inches along one of the end sections.

Other than a slashing from the knife of a would-be-thief at a music festival, I'd never suffered any kind of tent damage before. Consequently, I was only mildly prepared for such an issue. I dug out a roll of duct tape from my pack and sealed the crack thoroughly. After my stopover in the B&B at Ivybridge, I wouldn't be needing this tent anymore; a friend would be joining me for the first couple of days of my coastal trek and would be bringing my larger (and, regrettably, heavier) tent with him. Until then I was reliant on that duct tape – and the hope that no more animal-asses would come crashing down on me in the middle of the night.

As I departed Yennadon Down, heading south-east, the fog left behind a thick blanket of uninspiring clouds as it lifted, hovering not far above the rocky pinnacles of Sharpitor, Leather Tor and Sheepstor. Clinging to the last of their white blossom, hawthorn trees lined the edge of Yennadon Down. Occasionally the trees parted, affording me superb views across the water. For the first time I observed the reservoir almost in its entirety, and the grey sky failed to dilute the lush greens of the conifers along its perimeter.

Despite this view I couldn't help feeling slightly underwhelmed. But in fairness to the reservoir, this was due mostly to the weather – to which, along with those evasive ponies, I had attributed that morning's photographic failure. Now possibly facing another, I struggled to decide whether this scene was worthy of sacrificing a little more battery power. Based on the philosophy that if a shot was worth taking, then its validity would never need to be questioned, I ruled this one out.

Then I began to reconsider... Yes, the fog had destroyed any possibility of getting the shot I had envisaged, of the sun rising over the reservoir. But the view presented to me now, showcasing this foreboding sky, had potential for a striking black-and-white image. Why had I not realised this sooner? Evidently I still had some way to go in shaking off my preconceptions of what made a great photo.

Then, whilst composing my shot, I was struck by another idea. Included in the foreground, amongst the bracken that covered most of the hillside, were a few perky foxglove flowers. Their tiny, purple, bell-shaped blooms carried a lot of weight in this scene. On a brighter day, whilst they would have served as a worthy component of the shot, they would have blended into the landscape with little prominence against the pristine blues of the reservoir and sky. Now they provided a stark contrast to the shades of greys and greens that dominated the scene. Those flowers would be lost in a black-and-white photo. In the space of a few minutes, my shot had evolved from a reject, to rebirth in monochrome, to a symbol of my enlightenment as to what constitutes natural beauty.

Dartmoor was indeed teaching me a thing or two about photography.

At the bottom of the hill I left Yennadon Down, joining a narrow lane along the western edge of the reservoir, soon reaching Burrator Dam. This dam crossed a chasm aptly named Burrator Gorge, 110 metres across and 23 metres high. The five-year construction of the two dams on this reservoir began in 1893, and in 1929 they were raised by three metres to increase capacity to a whopping 4,210 mega-litres, making Burrator the largest of all Dartmoor's reservoirs.

Halfway across I paused to gaze over the edge, down to where the River Meavy emerged at the base of the southern side, cascading over a weir before disappearing amongst the trees downstream.

Across the dam, a thin strip of woodland separated the road from the reservoir before it passed the second dam – this one named after the nearby village of Sheepstor. This comparatively simple structure, consisting of a sloped earth embankment covered in concrete, ran notably longer than its partner – but without the supreme feature of height. The view across the water was no less pleasing, though. A few picnic benches furnished a lawn near the top of the dam. So, entertained by a few ducks and geese, I paused to take a break.

The road then left the reservoir behind, leading me through Sheepstor Village before turning off onto another lane, heading uphill for about a kilometre.

Panting furiously as the hill levelled off, I came to a junction opposite a gate at the roadside, where a signpost marked the start of a public bridleway. This weaved a vague line across the expanse of Ringmoor Down, matching the prominent dotted green line on the map that ran right up to Ditsworthy Warren House. The thick clouds that had failed to disperse all morning still filled the sky – now accompanied by a veil of mist suspended over the moorland ahead.

Seemingly, the mist had covertly pursued me all the way from Foggintor Quarry, revealing itself now and then to try and spoil my day. Well the mist had no chance – because this was just the kind of weather I'd been hoping for at Ditsworthy Warren. In the same way that misty conditions would have set the scene perfectly for my shots of Wistman's Wood, this weather was perfect for photographing mysterious old houses, too.

I turned around to scrutinize the grey buildings that constituted Sheepstor village, now some distance behind me. To their right climbed the tor of the same name, capping the hill of Yellowmead Down, which concealed most of Burrator Reservoir. My attention then fell to the road I was about to depart. I didn't expect to see another for three days.

Carrying more than a shred of trepidation about what these final days of my hike might bring me – but still fully intending to complete my planned route – I scanned the bleak, vacuous moorland ahead.

I opened the latch and tried to swing the gate open. The thick mud congealed around the bottom had other ideas, though. So, as the gate clattered and wobbled, almost sending me tumbling to the ground, I heaved my pack and myself over the top, then headed across the misty moor.

A series of anonymous wooden stakes waymarked the route, accompanied by the faint imprints of horseshoes. During my entire hike, this was so far only the third time I'd come across any kind of navigational assistance. But that was how it should be; I would have felt cheated had I left Okehampton to find waymarkers all over the place. I looked forward to the satisfaction of knowing I'd completed my journey aided by little more than my trusty map and compass.

I paused to glance behind me. Gone was the hedgerow bordering the road. To the south, on my right, the subtle undulations of the moor terminated my view a couple of miles away. In every other direction the moorland rolled on as far as the haze would permit. Soon the last sliver of Burrator Reservoir also disappeared. Sheeps Tor, scratching at the horizon about a mile to the north, now offered the only recognisable feature still in sight. Then that was gone, too.

The stakes led me eastward into a thickening mist, which merged seamlessly into low cloud, bringing a light drizzle with it.

After a while the moor dipped slightly and the grey line of a drystone wall began to emerge through the mist, followed by a dark splodge. Soon the splodge morphed into a building, decorated by a few tall trees within a walled garden: Ditsworthy Warren House.

From this distance the property seemed un-remarkable – but I carried high expectations of this place. Not long before departing for Dartmoor I'd seen the house captured on film in the Spielberg film *Warhorse* – so I was well aware of its affinity with the camera.

As the name suggests, this dwelling had been built to house the keeper of Ditsworthy Warren – once the largest commercial rabbit-breeding farm in England. Evidence of such activity can be found across Dartmoor, in the form of numerous long, cylindrical structures known as Pillow Mounds, which housed the bunnies. I had yet to discover any such features during my hike (then again, I wouldn't have had a clue what I was looking for. It was entirely possible that at some point I could have passed right by such a feature without even realising it).

There has been much debate over the age of this house, but parts of the structure are believed to date back to the sixteenth century. Successive families of rabbit-farmers occupied the property until its abandonment in 1947. Today, although still unoccupied, the house and grounds remain privately owned, and the building is often used – like much of Dartmoor – by the army, who lease it as a shelter for soldiers out on training exercises.

Reaching the drystone wall that bound the property, I never even considered that the land upon which it sat was not open access land. With no signage anywhere to indicate that the garden was private property, it wasn't until a close inspection of the map later that I spotted the faint yellow border that encircled the grounds, denoting their exception from public-access-land status. Neither was there anything to prevent my accessing the garden; the wooden gate on the western side of the wall had snapped off its hinges, quite some time ago judging by the state of it, and now stood leaning redundantly up against the wall.

On the front of the building, all seven windows had been boarded up by some black material, four on the upper floor and three on the lower, matching the colour of the roof. A chimney perched at the top of both gables, along with a much larger one between. A gated porch concealed the door. To the right of the house, another wall, as high as the upper floor windows, separated a small yard from the rest of the garden.

The grounds extended out from the house for 20 metres or so, decorated with a few trees – both deciduous and evergreen – and small piles of stones here and there. The wall frequently encroached into the garden to form small enclosures, which I guessed had once penned in livestock or pets.

The mist had blotted out the landscape beyond the house perfectly, enabling me to capture a very satisfying image from outside the broken gate.

Then, moments after I crossed the threshold of the garden, the drizzly rain turned into a pummelling downpour. I rushed over to a small building to the left of the house. Prompting a squeal from its rusty hinges, I swung the door open and took refuge inside.

Here I discovered the remnants of a white, plastic toilet-bowl, plugged with mud, whilst its detached seat leaned against the wall amongst various bits of junk. The distinct odour of sewage seeped up from a clogged wastepipe, along which scuttled a few bugs. A yellow, plastic bucket sat next to the bowl, containing a dirty rag and an aerosol can of some sort.

The stone walls were covered in the same flaking white paint as the door. Perched on a beam, between a rotting roof of plywood and the doorframe, was an abandoned bird's nest (or, to be precise, in the absence of any tweeting noises I could only assume it had been abandoned, since it was too high for me to peer inside). The musty odour of the roof mingled with that of the ageless effluent clogging up the wastepipe.

I wondered how much time had passed since this had been a functioning convenience. But I also struggled with the rationale that had led to the installation of a modern plastic toilet in the grounds of this quaint, Olde-English homestead. Surely a hole in the ground, or a bucket, would have been more appropriate?

I sheltered in there for maybe half an hour as rain pelted against the roof, producing a brain-drilling racket like that of popping corn mixed with radio static.

I then began to feel an urge swell within me. An urge I'd felt only once before over the past eleven days. An urge that overflowed with irony as I stood in that dilapidated toilet.

I needed a poo.

Despite the non-functioning toilet, this garden was actually not a bad place to go at all. At least here I would be relatively unexposed. And if anyone had told me before setting out on this hike that I wouldn't need to take a dump in the bushes until well into my second week, I would have pelted them with (unused) bog-roll.

Once the rain had stopped, I dug out my toilet roll, vacated the broken bog and dropped my pants alongside the wall near the bottom of the garden, well away from where any other visitors might tread after me – at least until long after Mother Nature had disposed of my stool, anyway. Until such a time, I would be adding only a minor contribution to the plentiful scatterings of sheep and rabbit poop all over the place.

I covered my steaming turd in wads of toilet paper, then buried the lot beneath a cute pile of stones, ensuring just enough paper poked out to advise any future hikers that my rudimentary pyramid was best left un-disturbed.

Whilst sanitising my hands, I stood back to admire my handiwork. I'd considered packing a trowel for moments like these, but had been forced to ditch it due to limited pack-space. But I won't deny that my aversion to the thought of burying my own shit had played some part in that decision. As I eyed the bits of paper poking out from between the stones, I couldn't help feeling a little guilty. But in my defence, there were no hard and fast rules on the Dartmoor National Park website detailing how one should deal with these eventualities; it merely requested that waste be dealt with 'sensibly and with care'. But I suppose, in retrospect, it could be argued that I hadn't fully considered the meaning of the wild camping mantra, 'Leave No Trace'.

Anyway, with that distraction dealt with, and as the rain began to patter on my jacket again, I began my detailed examination of the house.

The black sheets in place of the windows were actually hinged shutters. Behind the prison bars of the porch was a re-enforced door, bolted in three places. The bars had once been red, though now only patches of the paint remained as rust had taken hold. A few ferns sprouted from the stone floor behind, providing a vibrant slash of green against the pale granite and steel.

There were no rear windows or doors to the house; I supposed fire safety regulations were an alien concept at the time of its construction. The rear of the grounds boasted nothing of note, other than some large, cubic holes built into a thick section of the garden wall. Kennels, perhaps, or somewhere to which naughty little brats could be banished...?

After examining the house from a few other angles, I decided that my first photo was *the* photo. This location had certainly met my expectations, though, offering the perfect image of the quintessential Olde-English cottage, tinged with a mysterious solemnity.

I stepped back from the house, then turned around for one last look. I conjured up images of those who might have once lived here. An elderly yet self-assured widow, dressed in layers of tattered clothing, perched outside in her creaking rocking chair, watching the sun set on a cool autumnal evening. Whenever her gnarled, arthritic hands permitted, she spent her remaining days spinning yarn or chopping the heads off chickens. Waiting patiently to die but with a sure smile fixed upon her crumpled face. Nearby, her doting sons trained unruly horses with whips, or hammered shoes onto their hooves, preparing the animals for Mother's final ride.

Hopefully they'd sort that toilet out for her, too.

According to the map, the route to my next destination – Nun's Cross Farm – was unmistakeable: a prominent, almost straight path leading north-east from Ditsworthy Warren House, for a little over two miles, passing through a former tin-mining area to the left of another tor. The map showed a few other tracks heading towards the same point of interest, though none as significant as the bold, dotted green line that marked my desired route.

However, not all the routes visible *on the ground* quite matched those on the map. I therefore reasoned that I should simply take the most established one that followed a north-east direction. Follow that, and surely I couldn't go wrong. In any event, I was pleased to note the absence of any more wooden stakes to guide me; it was time to navigate on my own again.

The drizzle eased off as I got moving. Soon, a tiny cluster of rocks appeared at the top of a small hill to my right. That had to be the tor – offering sufficient reassurance that I was on the right path.

If I'd read the map correctly, the path would soon fork, where I would bear left. Taking the other route would still lead me to Nun's Cross, but would add an extra mile or so to the journey, as it linked up with a much longer footpath known as Abbots Way, before turning back towards the cross.

The fork never appeared. At least not to my eyes, anyway. Neither did I spot any old mining works. This didn't really matter, I supposed, as ultimately the paths would still lead me to Nun's Cross whichever route I took.

I soon forded a tiny stream – at a location that *unmistakably* matched the map. This told me that wherever the path had divided, I had taken the right fork. So, after little more than a kilometre this path would turn sharply to the left, then after about another kilometre I would reach the cross.

After trundling on for another half an hour or so – easily surpassing a kilometre – the path had *not* turned sharply to the left. Which meant I was heading further east, away from Nun's Cross Farm. A few other paths had converged with mine here and there along the way, but with none turning away on the bearing I'd expected, I'd stayed on course looking out for that sharp turn.

I turned back, scrutinising every little junction as I went. One such junction headed west up a gentle hill. It was by no means a perfect contender…but short of traipsing back to Ditsworthy Warren House and starting again, this was my best option.

Soon this path linked with a wider track, where my compass at last told me I was heading in the right direction. The path climbed teasingly as I waited, with trepidation, for the lonely Nun's Cross Farmhouse, or perhaps even the cross itself, to appear over the top of the hill.

I reached the top of the hill.

No house. No cross.

Ever-so-gently, the path began to descend. Minutes passed. Long minutes.

Then, in an otherwise tree-less world, a couple of evergreens appeared in the mid-distance.

I recalled the pictures I'd seen of Nun's Cross Farmhouse, flanked by a lone pine tree on either side. As I drew closer, my shifting perspective widened the gap between them, and a dark, solitary, grey building crept into view.

I puffed out my cheeks. Then allowed myself a smile.

A drystone wall marked the boundary of the property along most of its perimeter, save for a few man-made hillocks here and there, bolstered by some limp barbed wire. The house itself faced away from the path, appearing to be constructed not of the same granite blocks as the dwelling I'd surveyed earlier, but of some much darker, and frankly, uglier material. The tiled, weather-beaten roof sported a chimney at each end. A large outhouse backed the property, roofed with dirty sheets of corrugated metal. A rudimentary chimney, in the form of a tube, poked above the outhouse; an incongruous component of the property which, I assumed, had been added in more recent years.

A short distance from the house, the grey stone of Nun's Cross (or Siward's Cross, as it is also known) gradually distinguished itself from the path. Of all the ancient crosses across Dartmoor, this one is generally accepted to be the oldest, dating back to the thirteenth century, and photographing this monument further warranted my visit to the area.

My annoyance over my navigational blip waned as I reached the cross, but just as I was mulling over what kind of shot I could capture, with the moody cloud hanging low behind it, something caught my attention from the patch of land between the cross and the house. Numerous speckles of reds and blues dotted the terrain; alien stabs of colour amongst the muted shades of yellow and green moorland. Congregated within the grounds were about a dozen youths, dressed in bright raincoats, shooting arrows at a target. Drawing nearer, I noticed faint plumes of smoke emerging from the chimney of the outhouse.

For the second time, I was going to have to share my campsite. Oh well. Perhaps they would be gone soon...

Then I reminded myself of how I'd misjudged those youngsters at Foggintor. Nevertheless, right there and then those youths were spoiling the background of my next photo. So instead I turned my attention to finding somewhere to pitch.

Gone was the smooth grass that had accommodated me over the previous couple of nights; covering virtually all of this moorland were the spongy tussocks that I'd become well acquainted with earlier in my hike. But I also wanted to remain out of sight of those archers. I also needed to pitch quickly, for the bulging clouds overhead signalled another imminent downpour was approaching.

I followed a faint path, almost 90-degrees to the one that had brought me to the cross. It led me across a trench-scarred area, passing the ruins of a former tin mine and a concrete culvert, from which emerged a stream. Maybe this insignificant path actually corresponded to that well-marked one on the map – the one I should have followed from Ditsworthy Warren House? I could have tested this theory, of course, by seeing if the route would lead me back there. My curiosity didn't extend that far, though, so I turned back.

I inspected and rejected a few potential pitches before returning to the strongest contender – which lay only a few minutes' walk from the cross and still within sight of my neighbours. I conceded that I'd have to sacrifice a little privacy in return for a prime location from which to shoot my subjects. Once I had the house and cross to myself, of course.

Then, as I unclipped the tent from my pack, so began another hammering from above.

Wind and rain continued, unabated, throughout the evening. I peeked outside on a few occasions to check for any improvement. There was none. Unsurprisingly, the archers had retreated to the comfort of the house.

As darkness fell I reached for my headlamp to continue the latest chapter of my book. Something dripped onto my arm. I switched on the torch and glanced up. A patch of about a square foot of the flysheet was sagging against the inner tent, causing rain to seep through. Most of the ingress was running down the inside of the fabric – whilst a few less-patient drops were preparing to deposit themselves onto my sleeping bag. I assumed that in my haste to escape the rain I simply hadn't pitched the tent tightly enough: a schoolboy error that had compromised its rigidity against the wind.

Then I remembered that cracked pole.

The pole that had appeared to be in no worse condition when I'd examined it earlier. I studied the crack in the torchlight. Still the damage seemed minimal, yet there was a definite increase in the curvature of that section of pole. I wrapped more layers of duct tape around the offending area, then stepped outside for an inspection.

Something wasn't right. The tent was looking…deformed. In my rush to get out of the rain I simply hadn't noticed before. Yet everything was stretched and pegged correctly and as tightly as possible. As I fumbled with each peg and guy line in turn, through the clatter of rain came the faint sound of laughter emanating from the house. I imagined a party was in full swing. Perhaps with marshmallows being toasted over an open fire. And beer.

I made a few adjustments to the guy lines, in the hope that it might offer some improvement.

It didn't.

Chapter Ten: Best Laid Plans

The wind and rain slammed against my tent for most of the night, until the elements eventually took pity on me shortly before dawn and I squeezed in a precious couple of hours' kip, waking to a gentle breeze lapping playfully at the flysheet.

Were my neighbours still in residence at Nun's Cross Farmhouse? After waking up in their cosy, dry beds, were they now enjoying a full English breakfast at the kitchen table…?

I examined the wet patch of the inner tent. It appeared unchanged, though a few pools had accumulated at the edge of the groundsheet, behind my pillow of clothes.

I mopped up, then turned on the radio and waited for the weather forecast, enduring the same barrage of adverts for local shops, trades and services that had drilled into my brain for nearly two weeks. They reminded me of one of my favourite *X-Files* episodes – in which a sinister government agency uses subliminal messaging, hidden within the LED displays of electronic devices, to drive people insane. The story reaches its climax with an unhinged middle-aged salesman climbing to the top of a church tower with a hunting rifle, before the heroic FBI agents manage to persuade him to abandon his homicidal thoughts.

Although unable, quite, to describe my mood as optimistic, my emotional state stopped short of any desire to mimic such behaviour. Not even the cumbersome pony that had collapsed onto my tent a little over 24 hours ago – the most likely cause of my potential housing crisis – could incur my wrath.

The irritating jingles gave way to the news and weather as I forced down my porridge. The forecast was grim; heavy rain would be sweeping across Devon all day long. This was of little concern to me, though; my waterproofs hadn't failed me yet. I also told myself, again, how lucky I'd been with the weather throughout my hike. Even yesterday, when the downpours finally did arrive, the first coincided perfectly with my arrival at Ditsworthy Warren House – and its crumbling toilet. One could even argue that I'd been *too* lucky. In fact, I was almost hoping to face a deluge at some point, my philosophy being that this would complete the arc of contrasting weather conditions I would experience over my two weeks on Dartmoor. I still carried the physical stain of that first scorching week: my nose was *still* peeling, along with a few flaky patches on my neck, and, according to my camcorder, the redness of my face had barely faded at all. In a way, if I was to bid farewell to Dartmoor in a few days having not experienced an extreme contrast to those conditions, I would feel like something of a cheat.

A big downpour might also throw in a bit of excitement to what might otherwise be an uneventful penultimate day; after departing from Nun's Cross Farm I didn't expect to come across anything of note on the landscape until I reached the stone row on Stall Moor, near the Erme Plains valley. There are over 70 stone rows dotted across Dartmoor – but somehow I had yet to come across any of them. At 3,320 metres long (the longest *in the world*, allegedly) this one was surely unmissable. To reach the northern end of those stones, near to which I intended to camp that evening, I would be following Abbots Way, heading roughly south-east, for about five miles from Nun's Cross Farm.

The following day would consist of a short stroll south to Piles Copse – another ancient woodland. This cluster of old oaks sprang up along a stretch of the River Erme, roughly three miles north of Ivybridge. Like Foggintor Quarry, this place was revered as a great location for wild swimming. And whilst my earlier experience of Dartmoor's rivers told me to stay out of the water, I still intended to make this beauty spot my final overnight stop before reaching Ivybridge around lunchtime the day after. That would wrap up my time on Dartmoor nicely, and a few shots of each of those two locations would put the cherry on top.

The grass squelched beneath my feet as I headed over to explore Nun's Cross Farm and Siward's Cross. A mass of dark cloud was rolling in from the south, muscling in on the calm sea of grey over the house.

A herd of cows loitered nearby, eyeing me curiously, perhaps contemplating whether to trample my tent into the ground, as vengeance for my incursion onto their territory. My previous form with cattle – and ponies, now, too – suggested this was certainly not beyond the realms of possibility, but I dismissed the thought with a chuckle.

Looking beyond the cross, I saw no-one in the garden. Neither was there any smoke rising from the chimney. Aside from the rustling of my jacket in the breeze, once again the moor was deathly silent.

Alone at last.

I wasn't overawed at the sight of the cross up close. What first struck me was how little it actually bore the shape of a cross, being more like a thick pillar with a small obtrusion poking out from each side. It had also been broken in half at some point during its long history (during the 1840s, I later learned) and had been bolted back together by rusted metal clamps. It stood a fraction over two metres tall and, apart from a few white patches of lichen, carried the same grey hue as the dilapidated drystone wall behind it. The cross bore some weathered inscriptions, but the only one I could decipher was the word 'Syward' – a variation on the spelling of 'Siward' – the original name given to this landmark. Syward was the name of the Earl of Northumberland from the eleventh century AD, who had purchased land around Tavistock prior to the Norman Conquest. Concerning the alternative name of Nun's Cross, this is more of a mystery, as there is no historical evidence associating the cross with any nuns or nunnery. One possibility is that Nuns is a derivative of an old Cornu-Celtic word, 'Nans' – meaning valley. However, whilst the cross was located at a fractionally lower elevation than the surrounding moorland, I struggled to see how anyone could describe this area as a valley. Widely believed to have been erected sometime around 1240AD, the cross may have also been intended as another waymarker, for monks travelling between the abbeys of Tavistock and Buckfast. If that latter theory was correct, however, this would date the cross back by a further few hundred years.

Of the three crosses I'd visited, this was my least favourite. However, with the foreboding clouds beyond, and the rear of the moody house and the misplaced pine trees in the background, the cross was certainly still worthy of a photo.

Once satisfied with my shot I glanced back to check if my slightly insane theory about the cows destroying my tent had been realised. It hadn't. So, as they dithered on the track I wandered over to the house, giving a wide berth to a few less-sociable bovines lingering in solitary nearby.

I had seen no-one leave the house, which maintained its deathly silence as I approached. No snippets of conversation. No pans clunking in the kitchen sink.

The house was a stark contrast to the quaint buildings of Ditsworthy Warren – but, with its slightly sinister quality, was no less appealing, neither to the camera nor the imagination. Indicated by the absence of bricks, and its uniform, dark-grey walls, the house appeared to have been constructed of concrete. Whether or not concrete existed in 1871 I had no idea, or perhaps the original brickwork had been rendered later as part of restorative work. That seemed unlikely, though. Either way, this dreary house complimented the desolate moorland perfectly.

Nun's Cross Farmhouse was built in 1871 by a man named John Hooper – an enterprising farmer who leased this small holding from the Duchy of Cornwall. He reaped the rewards of a modestly successful cattle business until abandoning the property in the 1950s. The house is often credited as a source of inspiration for the author, Sir Arthur Conan Doyle, who based one of his most famous works – *The Hound of the Baskervilles* – on the tale of a ghostly canine that prowled Dartmoor after dark.

This house could have been the kind of place where escaped convicts would hide out. Or where crime warlords would have their henchmen interrogate and torture their enemies. No-one would hear the victim's screams for miles around. When the perpetrators were done, they would dispose of the bodies in a shallow grave somewhere out on the moor. In a bleak place like this, they could quite easily get away with it.

A porch with a dirty white door marked the entrance. Grey shutters and bars covered every window – of which there were two on the lower floor and three on the upper. One of the lower floor shutters bore a sign advertising the place as a bunkhouse for hire, complete with a few faded photos, showing a four-ring gas cooker (gas provided); a wood-burner (wood provided); a dining table with benches, and mattresses for the three upstairs bedrooms.

After exploring and taking a few shots, I filled my bottle in a stream and located Abbott's Way, then headed back to the tent with renewed enthusiasm – only for it to be dampened again when I observed, up close, just how compromised my tent had become.

The bending of the damaged pole had worsened, causing the height of the tent to dip by maybe five inches on the entrance side. The crack had extended a little, peeking out from beneath the layers of duct tape. Across the rest of the pole, the flysheet had shifted about eight inches from where it should have covered the top of the inner tent. Worst of all, despite the fly still being taut, almost half of its rear side was resting against the inner tent.

I packed up and dismantled my dodgy shelter, fearing the worst as I pulled the hook from the broken section of pole. To my surprise it remained in one piece. All I could do was wrap it in more tape.

Ten minutes later I was standing near the spot where I'd filled my bottle, close to the resumption of Abbots Way. With my map and compass close at hand and my waterproof jacket tied around my waist, I set off deeper into the bleak moorland, heading straight towards those even bleaker clouds.

The path began to climb a subtle ascent named as Crane Hill on the map. As I'd noted yesterday, Abbot's Way headed south-east then turned sharply to the right, about a kilometre from where I'd forded that stream. It would then gradually curl back round to head south-east again, in the direction of Erme Plains.

But what began as a muddy, well-worn route, pockmarked with the imprints of horseshoes, quickly dissipated into the faintest of lines across the rough terrain.

Soon the line was gone – with nothing in its place but the familiar tussocks. Every few minutes I paused to look back at the ever-shrinking farmhouse and its flanking trees, checking the compass to maintain my south-east heading. Already, my belief that I was still on Abbot's Way was almost gone. Nevertheless, at the point where I was sure I'd walked about a kilometre from the stream, I paused, scanning the area for anything I could interpret as a sharply-turning path. But there was no indication that any feet – human or otherwise – had ever crossed this ground.

No more than half an hour since leaving Nun's Cross Farm, I'd lost my bearings yet again.

I could have just gone back to the house and started again – but was that the way my journey would play out all the way to Ivybridge, with me backtracking to my last known location every time I lost a path? Every half an hour??? There was no doubt in my mind whatsoever that I had set off on Abbot's Way. The junction of the two paths near the cross were the only routes marked on the map – and they matched the map location and compass bearing *exactly*. From that moment, I had scrutinised every step ahead of me. How would I possibly end up in any better situation on a second attempt?

I was *not* going back.

Still believing to be reasonably close to the point where the path made that sharp turn, I adjusted my direction by 90-degrees and set off again, convinced that in a matter of minutes I'd find the path.

Then, inevitably, but still quickly enough to catch me off guard, the rain arrived. In torrents.

I crouched down to remove my pack and put on my waterproofs. I first tried to drag the trousers on without removing my boots, but their lining wouldn't stretch over the heels. If I'd been just a little more sensible, and hated them a little less, I would've put the trousers on earlier. I sat on my pack, cursing the hammering rain as I untied my boots and pulled them off...then dragged the trousers over my ankles...then put my boots back on...then tied the laces...then stood up and pulled the waterproofs up over the waist of my normal trousers. The wind had picked up and was slapping at my additional layer of clothes, competing in decibels with the rattling raindrops. Clinging to the hood of my jacket, I scoured the landscape in every direction. Nuns Cross Farmhouse was gone.

I had to push on. I considered taking the same approach as I'd adopted on Corn Ridge, forgetting about trying to follow paths and just heading in a straight line on my chosen bearing – in this case, south-east. In theory this would lead me to the stone row. But in addition to the obvious question of whether I would even see the stones from a distance, I knew only too well the kind of terrain I would face if I were to abandon the paths again.

But more importantly, at least to my pride, was the fact that I'd been traversing Dartmoor for almost two weeks, now. I wanted to believe that I'd learned to navigate my way out of these situations. Would I really have to revert to the desperate logic of following a straight line on a compass bearing? Walking in a straight line is what you do in a survival situation to escape from the wilderness (something else I'd watched Bear Grylls do many times).

But this was not a wilderness. Not really. Neither was I in a survival situation. Nothing terrible was going to happen if I didn't get to that stone row today. My only non-negotiable objective was to ensure I reached Ivybridge the day after tomorrow. All else was in the lap of the gods.

I set off again in search of that path, with the map now suspended from my neck in a waterproof cover, but tucked beneath my jacket to keep it from tangling around my neck in the wind.

The discovery of a well-defined track momentarily reassured me. Until my compass confirmed that instead of heading south-east as I'd hoped, this path headed due west. The path I sought meandered to some extent on the map, but at no point within a few miles of Nun's Cross did it head due west. So how could this be Abbot's Way? I stuck to my belief – and hope – that if I continued south-east across the tussocks, I would find the correct path and would be back on track. Quite literally.

My limp theory was bolstered when I took up another path, this time heading in my desired direction…only to soon turn sharply *away* from my desired direction; I was now heading north-east. I decided to stick with it and hope it changed course, or maybe joined with another route that would steer me the right way. If nothing else, at least I'd be off those tussocks and I could move at a decent pace.

On I went, monitoring my direction through my steamy, speckled glasses, keeping my eyes peeled as best I could for any junctions. The rain had found a path past my glasses and was trickling into my right eye, inducing a cool sensation somewhere between an itch and a tickle.

After a while the path converged with another, then curled around before heading south-east. Finally, I was heading the right way.

Then the path changed direction – again, unfavourably. Erme Plains was beginning to represent some kind of fabled promised land, within reach only with the aid of some fairy dust or magic shoes. I thought of those *Dorothy Gale* metaphors I'd conceived a few days ago, only now I imagined the *Wicked Campsite Receptionist of the West* watching over my woes through her cauldron, cackling with glee at my incompetence.

I paused to consider my next move. Without the underscoring thud of my boots on the path, the battering of the elements against my clothing made a fearful racket. I also sensed a growing dampness beneath my waterproofs, unsure if this was either rain seeping in or my trapped sweat clinging to my skin. Still gripping the hood of my jacket, I studied the hazy, raindrop-refracted view. A view unchanged in every direction since the moment that house had disappeared.

Finally I realised, without doubt, that navigating this network of paths was beyond my abilities. If I was to reach that stone row, my only hope was to revert to the amateurish, linear-walking method. Begrudgingly, I abandoned the path and began to negotiate the tussocks, again in a south-easterly direction.

I trudged on for what I guessed was about an hour, detouring around ditches and bogs wherever necessary. I crossed a couple more paths along the way, but since neither headed south-east I refused to let them steer me off course again.

Then, evidently unsatisfied with my current level of misery, the moor threw another ingredient into the brain-soup of my predicament: the stone row was on a bearing roughly south-east from Nun's Cross Farm – but that didn't necessarily mean that it was south-east *from my current location*. What if I'd wandered further south or west? If so, it was possible that I could actually be heading further *away* from the stones. Up until that point, all my decisions had been rationalised on the principal that if I kept moving south-east, I would eventually get to where I wanted to be.

Realising the flaw in that logic, more than a hint of panic set in. I imagined myself pitching up in some random location in the last light of day, then walking for miles to the nearest farmhouse the next morning, knocking on the door to foolishly enquire of its residents as to my whereabouts...and how to get to Ivybridge from wherever I was...

In a nutshell, I was lost. Probably no more than a couple of miles from Nun's Cross Farm. But still lost.

And yet...whilst my hopes of finding that stone row had taken a battering, they weren't *quite* dead. What had I learned was the best thing to do when trying to find your bearings? Go to high ground (yes – Bear Grylls had taught me this, too. He really was my hero).

I turned my back to the wind and fished out the map, wiping a film of condensation from the plastic cover – only for a smattering of raindrops to instantly replace it. My irritated eye squinted as I examined the contour lines twisting across the area I believed covered my present whereabouts.

I was drawn to two elevations. The aforementioned Crane Hill, from the bottom of which I'd departed Nun's Cross Farmhouse, and Green Hill. Virtually the same height, these two hills lay about a mile apart, their peaks in an almost perfect line heading south-east (yes, that impossible direction again) from Nun's Cross. The northern end of the stone row was about a mile south-south-east from the top of Green Hill.

I scanned the landscape for the two locations. However, the term 'hill' was proving something of a misnomer, since within a mile or two in every direction, the terrain varied in elevation by perhaps 20 metres at the most.

I then spotted an additional high point on the map: Great Gnat's Head, to the west of Green Hill, peaking at virtually the same height as the others. So now I was required to locate a triangle of hilltops. Well, that made everything so much easier…

I gazed around blindly as the rain continued to spray into my face. One hand clung to my hood, the other to the map as it flapped wildly in the wind. Unable to distinguish one hill from another, I heeded Bear's advice and simply headed up.

I plodded across the tussocks, climbing subtly but tediously as perspiration tickled the base of my spine. I had no doubt that my entire body was now soaked by an even mix of rain and sweat. Although I had seen no-one since the departure of the archers, I imagined fellow ramblers spying on me from the footpaths, highly amused at my ineptitude. At the same time, though, a part of me hoped to encounter *someone*, just so I might be pointed in the right direction.

Once the hill ceased climbing so did I. Surely I must have reached one of those three locations – but which??? I had been travelling mostly east from the cross. It was inconceivable that I could have gone far enough west to be at Great Knat's Head. Just as inconceivable was the thought that I could still be on Crane Hill – *the hill I'd started out from*. So, had I reached the top of Green Hill? I wanted to believe so, as this would mean I was just a mile or so from the northern end of the stone row. But as I'd considered already, even assuming I was on Green Hill, would those stones be prominent enough to find? And even if I found them, did I have it in me to find my way across whatever lay beyond…all the way to Ivybridge? These were massive questions. To which I had no answers.

I scanned the landscape desperately.

No stone row. Anywhere.

An experienced moorland explorer would have seen *something* useful. All I saw was a featureless, undulating sea of yellow and green, vanishing into a haze of mist and rain in every direction.

Enough was enough.

I checked the compass bearing that would hopefully take me back to Nun's Cross, then set off again.

My heart sank as I slogged along. Was I giving up too easily? If I'd read the map correctly, there could be no doubt that I'd reached the top of either Crane Hill or Green Hill. So if I just headed south-east from there I would come across the stone row eventually…right? But I was soaked to my skin, I could barely see through my glasses, and my confidence was shattered.

But to analyse the situation fairly, where I'd failed was in how I had read the land. The map was clear – and a compass never lies. I began to wonder how else I might get to that stone row, then told myself my focus needed to be fixed on getting back to Nun's Cross. Not only could I (probably) find my way off the moor from there, I could also camp there again if I hadn't the time, inclination or energy to walk any further before nightfall.

There was no sensible alternative. Not now that it had become clear that I was never going to find that stone row. Yes – I could carry on heading for *somewhere* near Erme Plains, and ultimately towards

Ivybridge, but where would I camp if I couldn't find those recommended camping spots at Erme Plains or Piles Copse? It would be a near-impossible task to pitch my defective tent on the tussock-covered terrain of these higher grounds, with maximum exposure to the wind.

Lumbering across the tussocks, I struggled to keep yet more questions from bubbling up inside my brain. Changes to my itinerary – major changes – were now almost inevitable. The only remotely-uplifting thought my brain could muster was the fact that the rain was easing off. A little.

Then a distant building began to creep through the haze, closely followed by two pine trees. As I drew nearer to them, the pure taste of the rain turned a little salty.

Every few minutes I glanced up, relieving my teary eyes from step-selection-duty, to instead observe the increasing definition of the trees; a pair of beacons upon a vast yellow ocean. As I drew nearer still, a sense of inadequacy replaced my relief, borne of the realisation that the location from which I'd turned back *was* Crane Hill – the closest of those two hills from Nun's Cross. I reached this conclusion after observing that the land did not rise and fall again between setting off from the top of the hill and my sighting of the house – so by the process of elimination it *had* to be Crane Hill.

My next realisation was even more of a shocker. I had meandered across the moor, on and off the paths, for over an hour. Yet, as the crow flies, I had ventured just over a mile from Nun's Cross.

One mile.

My feet squelched louder than ever, farting comically with each step as I reached the house. The rain had lost its torrential status, but still pattered vigorously against my clothes. The wind had also abated, to the point where I no longer needed to cling to the hood of my jacket. Like the rest of that item of clothing, though, the hood now seemed quite pointless.

Seeking shelter around the other side of the house, I sauntered past the poster that taunted me with its pictures of the mattresses and the wood burner blazing away. Rain gurgled along the guttering and down a broken drainpipe, emerging a few feet above the ground to splatter into a puddle before overflowing into the grass. I stooped down, letting my pack jerk me back against the side of the house, then I parked my backside on the stony ground. I stretched out my legs and watched in submission as raindrops plopped onto my saturated trousers.

I mulled over my options. There was clearly no waymarked route to the stone row – certainly not from its northern end, anyway (but despite my predicament, I would still be reticent to allow any of those emblazoned wooden stakes to guide me there). Attempting the same route I'd just failed at would surely turn out the same way. Or would it? I now knew about a third of the way for sure. I could retrace my steps back to the top of Crane Hill. From there I could follow the compass south-east, about a mile to the next high point of Green Hill, then head due south for another mile or so and I would hopefully come across the stones.

Aside from the inclusion of that torturous word, 'hopefully', breaking the journey down into those three stages made it sound so easy. Why hadn't I been able to do that an hour ago? Especially as I'd already identified that route up there. The stone row was literally *a few miles away.*

Then I reminded myself, again, that the stone row was *not* the finishing line of my hike...

The issue with the tent was also playing on my mind – although, in the grand scheme of things, that was of minor concern. If the worst really were to happen, the survival bag would house me for a couple of nights.

My mind drifted back to the days I spent planning my hike in blissful ignorance, pencilling in each stage of my journey on the map. I recalled those occasions during the first week that had tested my navigational skills – in areas with plenty of conspicuous landmarks. I'd just attempted to find my way over a mere couple of miles with no conspicuous landmarks – and had failed miserably.

In short, I was unprepared for this.

That was what my dilemma boiled down to – so after studying the map again, I made my decision and came up with a plan. I would still visit Piles Copse and Erme Plains – but I would have to take the long way round. A *really* long way round... First I'd head back to Yennadon Down for the night. The next morning I'd catch a bus from the nearest village, Dousland, into Yelverton, then another into Plymouth. From there I'd take a train to Ivybridge before rejoining the moor, taking the Two Moors Way to Piles Copse and the stone row. I'd camp somewhere at Erme Plains, then walk back into Ivybridge the following morning.

I despaired at the prospect of such a complicated, long-winded alternative route, lugging my pack about on more public transport. My intended hike would have been a mere ten miles or so over two days. This diversion was insane. But harder to stomach was my new-found sense of failure.

With the rain still pattering on my jacket, I hauled myself to my feet and studied the sky over Crane Hill. In place of that dark, bulging cloud was a great void of uncertainty, waiting to cast me adrift again on the yellow ocean.

I set off on the long walk back to Yennadon Down.

I assumed that would be the end of my navigational woes for the day. As it turned out, that little episode had shattered my map-reading skills completely, as I ended up unwittingly bypassing Ditsworthy Warren House on my way back to Sheepstor. Instead, I found myself on an alternate path heading further north across Ringmoor Down, bringing me to a car park at the end of a lane. By this point the rain had finally ceased, so I stopped for a break and another map-check. I also wrenched off those useless waterproofs.

That alternative route shaved a little time off my departure from Ringmoor Down, at least, and after passing through Sheepstor I revisited the reservoir. I made the most of my unexpected return by exploring a little more of its shores, leading to the discovery of a lovely waterfall in the woods near Burrator Dam.

I finally pitched at the top of Yennadon Down sometime around 7:00pm. Since I had no intention of leaving my tent that evening, I didn't bother seeking out the same spot I'd used 48 hours ago near the hawthorn tree.

I gritted my teeth and sucked in the air as I inserted the hook into that cracked section of pole. Again it survived the trauma – although it was now impossible to prevent the flysheet from touching the inner tent, right across its rear-end, so further leaks would be inevitable whenever it rained. Which would probably be quite soon. There was also a noticeable loss of headroom inside the tent.

But this was still my safe haven and I could at last strip off my sodden clothes, which clung to my skin as I tugged them off. After a rub-down with my towel I shoved my wet garments into a carrier bag, then sat cross-legged and naked on my warm, dry sleeping bag.

My body reeked of sweat, dirt, dampness and decay. To test the stickiness of my armpits, I performed something of a chicken imitation in slow motion. My skin peeled apart as if I were removing the backing from the Panini stickers I'd collected as a boy. I moved my legs in a similar fashion, producing the same sensation along the insides of my thighs.

I switched my focus to dinner, and soon the aroma of curry-flavoured rice was camouflaging my stench, with plumes of steam wafting up from the saucepan. As my rice bubbled away I began to reflect on the day's events with a wider perspective. At least I'd now completed that arc of weather experiences I'd been half-hoping for. As for my new itinerary, whilst a major pain, it would certainly eliminate the possibility of any further navigational blunders. My dodgy tent remained my only real problem. That was largely beyond my control anyway, so where was the sense in worrying about it?

Not even the discovery of another tick, this time on my leg, was going to spoil my evening. This bad-boy was maybe half a centimetre long – bigger than the previous one I'd played host to. But there would be no messing about this time. After wolfing down my dinner I set to work with the tweezers. To my amazement, the thing came out on the first attempt, and in one piece.

I tossed the bug outside, zipped up the tent, and snuggled into my sleeping bag. In the morning I would re-assess that pole and pay close attention to the weather forecast – and trust a little to luck. Piles Copse and the stone row were determined to elude me. But I wasn't beaten yet.

Then began a comforting, familiar pattering on the tent.

Heavy rain awakened me in the middle of the night. Not quite with the deluge that had lashed me about 12 hours earlier, but I knew within minutes that I would not be getting back to sleep.

I was content just to doze. Perhaps the rain and cloud would lift sufficiently by morning to allow me an alternative photo of that view over Burrator Reservoir. Perhaps I'd been fated to return here for such a purpose. It was a romantic notion, but also a misplaced one; those kind of images simply didn't belong here. This was a landscape of moody contemplation. Crossing it was to walk a tightrope between serenity and bleakness; fortitude and foolhardiness; solitude and intimacy. Dartmoor is an enigma; a forbidding yet ethereal rocky plateau, that sits and waits patiently on the roof of England's south-western peninsular, ready to seduce anyone who ventures within. The enigma will no doubt draw me back someday. Back into its consoling emptiness. An emptiness that, despite the challenges and confusion it had thrown at me, had proved as beautiful as it had intoxicating.

As I dozed to the waves of pounding rain, visions of the past two weeks wafted through my mind like swirling clouds of cinnamon. The ponies dancing near Brat Tor. The dawn mist over Meldon Reservoir. Being transported to another world at Wistman's Wood. My frustrating yet thrilling attempt to photograph the lightning over Foggintor Quarry. And I had only really scratched the surface of Dartmoor. Or, to be accurate, stumbled and squelched across it.

My reverie was interrupted by a drop of water landing on my head. I shouldn't have been surprised...but I was. I strapped on my headlamp and glanced up at the glistening surface above. A few raindrops were clinging to the inner tent, about to fall, but more were accumulating at the edge of the groundsheet. I fished out my toilet roll – my stocks of which were finally starting to dwindle – and soaked up the pools.

The rain eased around 9:00am, by which time the morning light had revealed the damaged tent pole bending even further beneath those useless layers of duct tape. That possibility of having to use the survival bag was inching closer.

Peering behind my pillow, I discovered fresh puddles. My renewed defiance of the elements waned after tossing yet more soggy toilet roll into my rubbish bag. I couldn't face spending hours on end out in the rain again. Especially in the knowledge that my waterproofs were, in fact, not very waterproof after all. The only garment in my pack that remained both clean *and* dry was a single sock. I'd lost its partner in a tumble-dryer at the campsite launderette.

I began to question my plans again. With my enthusiasm slipping away, and as the rain continued unabated, I waited, passing the time with John Lydon. I had no timetables for the bus and train services required to get to Ivybridge, but even if I didn't get back onto the moor until the late-afternoon, from there it would be only a couple of hours' walk to Piles Copse.

Eventually the rain stopped. Then the weather forecast announced a warning for 'heavy rain across the majority of Devon until nightfall'.

This was the endorsement I'd been waiting for. The endorsement to the decision that had been chafing at my adventurous spirit all morning.

My trek across Dartmoor was over.

The next time I would pack up, it would be to head for The Sportsman's Inn, Ivybridge.

A part of me conceded that I'd given up. But on balance I was sure my decision was the right one. Aside from the practical issues I faced, I realised that I'd seen and experienced all I'd needed to of Dartmoor. As for my photos, my hike had instilled another realisation in me: that the beauty of nature extended way beyond the cliché images I'd envisaged before my arrival at Okehampton. *My* photos documented *my* journey.

Those were the only photos I needed.

I spent that day alternating between the radio and my book. Heavy bursts of rain came and went. I ventured outside only once, to fetch water late in the afternoon. Without the aid of my guiding tree, and at no surprise at all, the return journey took a little longer than it had done previously. But as I strolled back up the hill, the clouds broke a few miles to the south. Sunbeams glided across the sky, spraying a milky glow over the landscape. The nearby ponies began to trot with a little more gusto, perhaps willing the sunbeams to pass over us. Perhaps willing my legs to power me up the hill faster as I raced to the tent to grab my camera, before those sunbeams could disappear.

Under the watchful eyes of my equine friends, I stood and stared across the moor expectantly. The clouds defied the calls of the ponies, depriving Yennadon Down of those enlightening rays. Within minutes, they were gone. But not without gifting me one more photo of Dartmoor.

Later, the clouds would also pass judgement over whether I was worthy of watching the sun set one last time on Dartmoor. As the evening drew in it became evident that in their eyes, I was not.

I didn't mind; that photo was enough.

The following morning I departed the moor for the last time. As a parting gesture the landscape threw a final navigational blip at me, initially sending me in the wrong direction across Yennadon Down on my way to the village of Dousland. My concentration had been sapped over those final two days, but eventually my boots touched tarmac, then carried me to the village bus stop.

Whilst waiting for my ride I summarised my adventure to a chatty, white-haired old lady, who seemed inquisitive but not particularly surprised to hear of my activities on the moor. She chuckled when I told her about the premature ending to my hike.

'So were you navigating by map or compass?' she asked.

'Both,' I replied, grinning unashamedly.

I had much to learn about hiking – and wild camping. That had become clear over the past two weeks – but I owned the mistakes I'd made. And I maintained my justification of my feeble daily mileages. As I'd stated at the outset of my journey, I hadn't come here to kill myself. I had come here simply to discover Dartmoor. Although I didn't quite realise it at the time, I had also begun to re-discover myself.

What surely *was* remarkable about the physical aspect of my hike, was the fact that throughout those entire two weeks, only twice had I been required to empty my bowels.

I spared the old dear from that little anecdote, though.

Two buses and a train ride later, I sprawled naked across the huge bed in my room at The Sportsman's Inn. After taking the longest shower of my life, I gorged myself on junk food – washed down with cold cans of locally brewed cider – whilst purging my frazzled brain with daytime TV.

The next morning I would visit a launderette (hopefully without losing any more socks), then meet up with my buddy and exchange my forlorn tent. Then I would be heading for the coast – to begin a ten-day hike along one of the most demanding stretches of the South-West Coastal Path.

What could possibly go wrong...?

Epilogue: A Question Answered

'Are you playin' Pokémon Go?' It was the most amusing question posed of me in quite some time, prompting a chuckle as I stood at the edge of the River Teme, just outside the city limits of Worcester – my hometown. I'd just removed my earphones after pausing the recording of a U2 concert on my phone, so I could appreciate the sound of water rushing over the weir at this energetic stretch of the river.

'No,' I replied, shooting a sideways glance towards the lad on my right, who'd been elected chief inquisitor by his gang of half a dozen or so pals. They hung back a few metres behind him. None of them could have been more than 13 years old.

'What are you doin', then?' the inquisitor demanded, in an abrupt tone that still managed to retain a sufficient level of politeness – the kind of tone that could only be delivered by the voice of a child.

I shook my head dismissively, winding the cord of my earbuds around my phone before returning it to my pocket. 'Just enjoying a stroll along the river,' I told him.

He nodded towards the calm water upstream of the weir. 'Are you gettin' in?' He'd phrased the question more like a command. I studied the spot he'd referred to, observing the almost sedentary current liven up as it trickled over a strip of concrete before gushing down a smooth slope a few metres away, foaming at the bottom and swirling through clumps of rocks.

Low water levels exposed much of this weir during the summer months. This year had been no exception; the United Kingdom had been basking – and wilting – in the longest heatwave to hit the country since the infamous summer of 1976. Satellite images had revealed our green and pleasant land turning brown and withered; farmers warned of impending food shortages because of poor crop yields; wildfires had ravaged the peat-covered moorlands of northern England, and depleted reservoirs prompted threats of hosepipe bans in parts of the UK. On the plus-side, coastal resorts were enjoying a boom in business as holidaymakers snubbed exotic overseas destinations, flocking to our own seaside instead.

Tragically, though, there had also been several drownings across the country. Nearly every week, it seemed, the media was warning of the dangers of swimming in open water, or reporting cases of youngsters who'd lost their lives after getting into difficulty in lakes and rivers.

These kids had no doubt been drawn to this little beauty spot for a swim, too. Most of them had removed their shoes and socks. A couple were topless. Perhaps unsure whether to commit themselves to the water, they'd stood lingering on the riverbank, beneath the shade of birch and willow trees, as I'd approached the weir. Further downstream I'd passed other bathers congregated along a tiny beach. Spread out across the sand were towels, picnic supplies, and a half-empty crate of beers. A hazardous combination of elements in a deceptively idyllic-looking setting.

But following my antics in the River Tavy two summers before, who was I to lecture anyone on the dangers of open water? At least these kids carried the reckless spirit of youth in their defence. In discouraging them from swimming here I would be a hypocrite. On the other hand, my cautionary tale could serve as a warning. But regarding this lad's question as to whether I would be entering the water, I maintained my poker face – even though he seemed to be reading my mind.

'Nope,' I replied, glancing back at him. The blank expression on his face suggested he was now at a loss as to the purpose of my visit. I suddenly thought of a diversion, nodding towards the makeshift road of wooden planks that had recently been lain not far from the riverbank, following a substantial scrub-clearing and ground-levelling exercise. 'Do you know what's going on, there? Are they building a road or something?'

'It's not a road...it's for trucks to get down 'ere. They're gettin' rid of the weir.'

'Getting rid of it? Why?'

'So the fish can swim back up the river.'

'Oh...right.' I was a little bemused – and, assuming this was true, rather disappointed. Although not particularly photogenic at this time of year, during autumn the weir offered decent camera opportunities – the higher water level allowing for some artistic long-exposure shots as the water weaved amongst the leaf-decorated rocks. The weir also faced east, so was perfectly placed for capturing mist over the water at sunrise.

'So you definitely ain't goin' in, then?' the lad persisted.

Now I was being dared. I couldn't help but grin in recognition of his spirit, then stepped back up onto the riverbank from the edge of the weir.

'Nah, not me...' I noted how un-convincing the words sounded as they exited my mouth.

'Why not?'

As spirited as this kid was, it was time to get out of this conversation. I headed for the resumption of the path at the end of the makeshift track, then offered a simple get-out-clause in answer to his question.

'Well for one thing, I can't swim.' Inwardly I reminded myself that this statement wasn't entirely true. Well, I was *fairly* sure it wasn't, anyway... 'See ya later!' I added.

'I'll give you two-hundred quid if you jump in the river!' one of the other boys shouted, much to the amusement of his pals. I glanced back, offering another grin and a shake of the head, then I left them to it and proceeded along the narrow path.

Clusters of Great Willow Herb, adorned with their tell-tale

purple flowers, dwarfed the dirt-track on both sides. A healthy population of nettles also called this place home. It was impossible to dodge them completely, resulting in one or two stings to my bare lower-legs. Then the path opened out into another clearing, passing by the graffiti-covered, concrete struts of Worcester's western bypass road, which bridged the river to my right.

On the other side of the clearing, the swathes of trees and shrubs returned, thankfully with fewer nettles, but still concealing the now-silent river from view. The hum of traffic from the road also faded away. Minutes later I crossed a rickety stile onto smooth, open pasture. The path now ran right alongside the almost cliff-like riverbank as it snaked through a meadow.

This was a route I'd taken many times – day and night. Sometimes with my camera or sometimes just to enjoy a peaceful countryside stroll, the start of which being only an hour's walk from my flat in the city centre. But this time I intended going only a few hundred metres further, to a beautiful little spot that I hoped had been overlooked by bathers. A spot where I could finally answer a question that had been smouldering away, deep in the recesses of my brain, for 14 years.

During the writing of this book, that question had been ignited – particularly whilst recalling my stay at the Harford Bridge Campsite. Now the time had come to extinguish the flames.

But that wasn't all my wild camping experience had ignited; it had awakened me from the comatose state in which I had lived much of my adult life. A few months after discovering Dartmoor I was discovering Cambodia – on my first overseas holiday since the days of those swimming lessons in Thailand. It was also only the fourth time I'd flown in my entire life. Other adventures have since followed – and more are rattling around inside my head. Adventures either too great in number or too bold in ambition for them all to be fulfilled, but at least some of those seeds will bear fruit. The fruit may not always taste sweet, but at least the flesh will be firm. Draw from that analogy what you will, but I think it means that my Traits-

Triangle now binds together just a little more robustly. Though I must confess that I have yet to be tempted to have another go at wild camping…

As I followed the next bend in the river I heard splashing. Peering through the trees, I identified a human head – probably male – poking above the water. Thankfully its body followed a moment later, leaning into a backstroke. The swimmer appeared to be alone – until I spotted a dog sat panting on the opposite riverbank. Their presence wasn't sufficient to dash my hopes of finding my spot deserted, so on I went.

The river curled round again at the edge of the meadow, where I crossed another stile. Then I left the path for the riverbank, where the grass dropped away into a beachy cove, about three metres below the field. The beach – and anyone on it – would go unnoticed by any passers-by unless they came right up to the edge of the meadow. The thick line of trees on the opposite bank would shield me from view on that side, too.

I scuttled down onto the beach, into its merciful shade. The stench of a few semi-fresh cowpats was the only blight on an otherwise perfect setting.

I stripped off, exchanging my heavy, combat-style shorts for a much lighter pair from my backpack, then proceeded to the river's edge, wincing as my naked feet pressed into the coarse, warm gravel.

The sandy riverbed succumbed slightly to my weight as I stepped into the water and edged my way out, bypassing the occasional rock beneath the surface. Long strands of some aquatic plant tussled with the current here and there, brushing against my legs. Then the water reached my waist.

Something made a loud splash downstream…the man and his dog? Was he getting *out* of the river? I paused for a few minutes in case he or anyone else came wandering along the bank.

Once reassured of my privacy, I waded in further, allowing the water to reach my shoulders. Compared to the coolness of my submerged skin, the heat of the unrelenting sun on the back of my neck seemed to multiply.

As I had done the last time I'd indulged in this activity, I bobbed up and down, observing shoals of minnows darting around me. But what I had not seen on the River Tavy were dragonflies. Here they were everywhere, flitting to and fro above the surface. I'd glimpsed them fluttering about whilst wading in, but it wasn't until now, with my eyes level with theirs, that I could fully appreciate their brilliant flashes of neon as they skirted above the shimmering water. Occasionally they landed on drifting leaf litter, sometimes in pairs, where they would bask in the sun for a few moments before taking to the air again. Once or twice they passed right by my ears, their wings buzzing like tiny chainsaws.

I began to rehearse my movements in anticipation of a breaststroke. Working up a rhythm, I directed the water either side of my body, simultaneously pressing my feet into the riverbed, resisting the pull forward with each stroke.

As the dragonflies continued to dart around me, I gradually increased the strength of my strokes. Soon I would be unable to resist that pull. I silently counted down on the next trio of moves.

On the third stroke I pushed forward with my feet. Unable to co-ordinate my upper and lower limbs, the lower ones flailed. I struggled to keep my head above the water, and after a few seconds I lost my nerve (or came to my senses, whichever you prefer). I grappled at the riverbed, bringing myself to a halt, before realising I'd propelled myself about a metre through the water.

I brought my feet back down to the pebbles, steadying myself, then took a moment to assess that first attempt. My arm movements, whilst lacking in finesse, were just about sufficient. Now I just had to focus on what my legs were doing.

Again, I counted down and pushed off on the third stroke, coiling my legs in towards my waist before kicking them out in a fanning motion. I sensed my body shift through the water as I repeated the process – this time with a little more conviction.

My moves were clumsy and my timing left much to be desired.

Some strokes took me further than others, but each carried me a fraction closer to the beach. The sunlight and the dragonflies continued their dance on the water's surface, beckoning me to the warm pebbles. A few seconds more and my hands would reach them.

Had anyone come strolling along the riverbank at that moment, they would have surely found this scene highly entertaining. Or highly concerning.

I didn't care; I was swimming.

About the Author

Mark Newman resides in the beautiful city of Worcester, in the heart of England, where he has lived all of his life. Whilst he drifts through a sterile world of dead-end jobs, he fantasises about an alternative existence that might offer a modicum of fulfilment. The rest of his time is mostly spent either writing or out and about with his camera. He also enjoys watching movies, comedy box sets and the *X-Files*. In addition to his love of camping, Mark is a keen armchair traveller – occasionally indulging in the real thing whenever time and finances permit. Mark's other big passion is music; he plays guitar, keyboard and harmonica, and has also been known to sing in public on occasion. Apparently he was never destined to become a rock star – but he still uses his musical skills to produce the soundtracks to his travel videos. *A Stroll on the Moors* is Mark's only book to date. Unless the midlife crisis really kicks in, there will be others.

Search 'Mark Newman Dartmoor' on YouTube to view the video diary that inspired this book. Actually, his YouTube channel hosts a whole plethora of audio-visual entertainment. It won't change your life…but there are worse ways to kill a spare half-hour.

A Stroll on the Moors is also available in a First Edition, featuring over 40 colour photos and colour artwork. You can also view Mark's Dartmoor photos (and many more besides) by visiting these social media pages:
www.facebook.com/MarkNewmanClicks
www.facebook.com/MarkNewmanScribbles

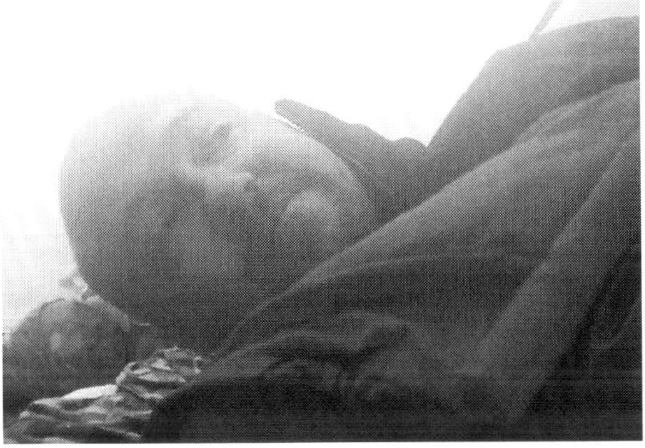

Printed in Great Britain
by Amazon